WATCHING WILDLIFE

WATCHING WILDLIFE

Ian Russell and Alan Major

BOOK CLUB ASSOCIATES
London

This edition published in 1983 by
Book Club Associates
by arrangement with
David & Charles (Publishers) Limited

© David & Charles 1983

Typeset by Monospools (Exeter)
Printed in Great Britain
by A. Wheaton & Co., Exeter
for David & Charles (Publishers) Limited
Brunel House Newton Abbot Devon

Published in the United States of America
by David & Charles Inc
North Pomfret Vermont 05053 USA

CONTENTS

INTRODUCTION

On a recent visit to my mother I awoke in the early morning and looked out of the window. There, sitting in the middle of the lawn, was a fox, quite at home and unconcerned. For the next half-hour it stayed there, scratching and grooming itself, until the bark of a dog disturbed it. This garden was not in the depths of the country, but in a busy suburb less than ten miles from the centre of London. Nor was this an isolated occurrence — foxes can often be seen there, late at night or early in the morning.

There could be no better illustration of how some wildlife can flourish in unlikely places. Keep an eye open for animals and plants, for they are almost everywhere. You may not have foxes using your garden, but there are many smaller creatures waiting to be discovered. Even in an apparently barren backyard there are things to be found, and if you have no garden at all there are usually parks within visiting distance.

This book is about those animals and plants that live in familiar places close at hand, or in places that we travel through in our everyday lives, or visit on our holidays. It is not concerned with rarities which inhabit wild moors and mountaintops, but with living things that are always around us.

Once we begin to look hard the variety is almost unbelievable. Most competent naturalists could put a name to only a fraction of the creatures to be found in an average garden as there is an army of insects, many small and often unnoticed, and a long list of microscopic organisms. There is no shortage of material for those who become interested, for we know surprisingly little about the habits of a large number of species. Many of us, though, do not need the stimulus of making new discoveries to enjoy wildlife. We are content to learn the names and habits of the plants and animals around us, and enjoy watching them through the changing seasons.

This book has been designed for people who want to do this. It covers four kinds of habitat and introduces the main types of animals and plants to be found, with suggestions of how and where to look for them. There are practical hints on how to encourage wildlife, and, where appropriate, there are tips on how to capture small creatures for study and how to keep them in good health. There are also

6

some ideas on investigating living things in the wild. Mostly, however, the emphasis is on finding, recognising and watching the wildlife of familiar places.

A huge acreage of Britain is now devoted to gardens, making this habitat one of the largest and most important for wildlife — and one that keeps growing. Even though some gardens are subdivided and built over, new houses with gardens are being built all the time. Gardens vary in their usefulness to wildlife. A neat 'well-tended' garden may offer far fewer opportunities than an untidy overgrown garden in which there is cover to hide, places to nest, a variety of food, and, perhaps most important of all, freedom from interference. Animals and plants cannot flourish where they are allowed no living space. The tidiest gardens can be nearly as barren of wildlife as a modern arable field. Such a field is ploughed, sprayed and given fertiliser in order to encourage a crop and suppress competition, which means most wild plants. There can be few places less hospitable to a variety of wildlife.

The lesson is clear. If we want plenty of wildlife in the garden we must cut spraying to a minimum and not be too fussy about weeding and tidying up. In practice, of course, not many people want a garden that has completely gone wild. They want to use the garden for growing vegetables or flowers, for playing in, or just as somewhere pleasant to sit. But a compromise can be reached, using the garden for your needs, but leaving odd corners which are hardly ever disturbed.

My garden is rather like this. We grow a few vegetables and have a small lawn and flower border. There are two small chicken runs, a few small shrubs, and one large pear tree at the far end. Between the shrubs and the chicken run, and in odd corners by the fence, we let anything grow that springs up, and only prune back plants which encroach on the lawn. This does no harm. Our garden suffers no more, and often less, from 'pests' than others down the road. Bindweed and bramble grow, but are not out of hand, and help to attract insects that might otherwise not visit. It is interesting to see what plants pop up in the garden without being planted by us, and to speculate on their origin. Holly, honeysuckle and gooseberry have grown, presumably spread by birds. We wait to see which wild plant is going to be 'plant of the year'. Last year it was nipplewort which appeared in abundance. This year, black nightshade, not seen here for at least ten years, has produced a mammoth crop in a neglected corner.

Some flowers we plant are meant to attract butterflies, and so they do, (although in town three or four species provide nearly all the visitors) but the range of bumble bees and hoverflies to be seen on a sunny summer's day is amazing. Some of the small garden inhabitants are only visible at night. We have a pet slow-worm, and on warm damp nights we go into the garden looking for slugs on which to feed him. Crawling about your gardens at night with a torch is apt to make

7

neighbours give you funny looks, but if you do go on a slug hunt you will be amazed how many there are. In the day they are mostly underground, but on a damp night legions of them are gliding round the garden, enough to give many gardeners a fit. In fact, most do very little harm at all in the garden, devoting their energies to feeding on vegetation which is already rotting. Worms are also much in evidence on damp nights, coming above ground to mate or pull vegetation into their burrows.

We do not encourage birds to feed in our garden (there are too many cats in the neighbourhood and the garden is not big enough to support a resident population), but a tit's nestbox placed safely out of reach is usually occupied in summer. The shrubs and trees attract plenty of visitors — we have seen treecreepers and firecrests. Squirrels come only rarely, it is too built up and there are not enough trees, but the road supports a large population of hedgehogs, and there are other small mammals including woodmice, house mice and voles. Most of these go unnoticed unless you are prepared to patrol the garden in the dark, or have a cat who will bring them to your attention.

This garden is a constant source of interest and sometimes education. I had always thought of dragonflies as being very much insects of bright sunlight until I saw some one evening, well after sunset, pursuing and catching cockchafers which were flying around the old pear tree.

By now you may be thinking mistakenly that we must have an enormous garden to have these hordes of creatures. From the house to the end of the garden is about 40 ft, and we are in the middle of a town. If you have a garden of your own, big or small, there is bound to be plenty in it for you to investigate. If you have no garden, perhaps there is a park near you. Again, the less regimented it is the more wildlife there is likely to be. Large parks may even have the space, and the quiet corners, for a badger sett or fox earth. One of the best park-like habitats for wildlife is an old cemetery. This can be a haven for lichens (growing on the stones), slow-worms and nesting birds. Many parks or gardens provide a habitat with some of the characteristics of woodland edges or clearings, allowing birds which like these conditions, such as the blackbird, to become much more numerous than in the past.

Gardens are important for wildlife in other ways. They provide a refuge for some aquatic species whose previous habitat has disappeared. The garden pond has enjoyed a surge of popularity, as the natural and man-made ponds of our farmlands have decreased dramatically. No longer used to water cattle, many disappear in drainage schemes or are filled in to enlarge fields or tidy up the farm. Fens and other wetlands have also been drained and the loss of habitat and suitable breeding sites has been disastrous for our amphibians. The common frog is no longer at all common over much of the country, and toads and newts have also decreased. So the ponds in our gardens, parks and commons have become vital as a reservoir of breeding stock.

In addition to ponds that are deliberately filled in, others suffer from vandals and dumpers of rubbish. Old motor oil can cause terrible damage. Streams, too, can be polluted so much that their life disappears. But all is not lost — even waters that have been polluted can be made clean again, and most people will be able to find a clean pond or stream within reach, in a park or on a local common.

Water always seems attractive, and certainly there is plenty to find there, but perhaps the real fascination is its mystery — you are never quite sure what you will find until you pull out your net. What emerges differs from week to week and year to year, even with the time of day. Most small children enjoy pond dipping; so do adults when they have children of their own as an excuse. Nothing can then prevent them from swelling the catch of newts, sticklebacks, leeches and water boatmen.

The static appearance of a pond on a summer's day is an illusion — it is seething with life. If it is shallow, plants will be rooted across its whole width and many animals will be hidden among them. It is a fertile world, but at the same time a very changeable one. Warm or dry weather lowers the water level, wet weather raises it again. In summer the water may become very warm and hold little oxygen; in winter the surface may freeze (although only the shallowest ponds freeze solid). One can only

admire the way the animals and plants adapt to the changes. In the long term, though, their world is doomed — the natural progression for a pond is for it to disappear. Plants in the shallows trap silt and debris round their roots and this slowly builds up until what was shallow water becomes dry land. Thus, the pond edges gradually move towards the centre. It may take a long time, but unless the pond is dredged or renewed it will eventually disappear. Go out and make the most of it while it is still there!

Of course, most habitats are changing, either naturally or because of the way man changes the countryside. One type of habitat that has seen much change over the last few hundred years is that of the waysides and hedges. Some parts of the countryside have had hedges for nearly a thousand years, but in others the field hedges are comparatively recent, dating from the great enclosures of the eighteenth century when former common lands were split into fields and fenced. The new hedges provided refuge for some of the animals and plants whose woodland home was being gradually removed.

Now the pendulum has swung the other way again. In some counties hedges have been subjected to wholesale removal to enlarge fields to make it easier to use large agricultural machinery. Luckily the process seems to have slowed down in recent years so there is hope that hedges will remain a familiar part of the landscape. But owners and councils who care more for neatness than ecology can still wreak havoc by mechanical hedge-chopping or by spraying verges. One of the few benefits of recent financial stringency has been that councils have cut out many unnecessary tidying up operations.

We still have many hedgerows that are full of interest, with literally hundreds of different plants. The hedgerow is an important means of plant dispersal; it also makes a highway for small animals such as voles and shrews, and acts as cover for woodland animals crossing open country. Hedges provide food and shelter for innumerable animals, and it has been calculated that in summer there may be as many as ten million pairs of birds nesting in hedgerows throughout Britain.

One interesting aspect of hedges is the differences between their two sides. There are often marked differences in a hedge that runs from east to west. The north side is damp and shady; woodlice or snails may flourish, and plants such as black bryony prefer these conditions. On the south side conditions are sunny and dry; butterflies, beetles, hoverflies and some spiders may be conspicuous. The west and east sides of a hedge running north/south may also offer different conditions.

You can calculate how old a hedge is by doing a hedgerow survey. (The chapter on hedgerow habitat tells you how). You can discover what plants grow there and make note of any animals you find. You can look for differences between the sides of the hedge, and see whether there are ditches on one or both sides with particular plants near them. If you go on holiday to different parts of the country you can compare the hedges there with those near your home. This is one sort of natural history that can be studied on the move, as even from a car it is possible to observe which types of plants are prominent in the hedge.

Holidays are the only time when most of us will have the opportunity to visit the habitat described in the fourth section of this book, the seashore. This is one of the most complex and rich habitats we have, and the forms of life found there can enthrall anyone from a professional biologist down to the youngest child. On some shores it is difficult to see life; a shingle shore shifts too much for life to become established; a sandy or muddy shore teems with life, but most of it is underground when the tide is out. But anyone, with no special equipment, just their own eyes and hands, can discover a myriad of treasures on a rocky shore by looking in the pools and on the rocks. The animals and plants are quite different to those on the land. Some appear bizarre to us, some are breathtakingly beautiful. Patient searching and a little skill with net and bucket may bring more rewards. As with other habitats the catch will vary with season but there is always something of interest and always the possibility of finding something you have not seen before.

The best seashore hunting is often done by following the tide down, searching the edge of the sea before

10

the inhabitants scuttle lower down or into hiding places to await the return of the tide. It is worth consulting the tide tables to discover the best days and time for your seashore hunt. If you can find a day with a low spring tide you will be in luck, as creatures will be revealed at the lowest tide that are never seen higher on the beach. But beware when searching — it is possible to become so absorbed that you do not notice the turn of the tide. Keep a lookout and an eye on your line of retreat. Also watch out for sun- and windburn. Both are particularly violent right by the sea and may not be noticed until it is too late. It is generally wiser when rock-pooling to be clothed and to wear non-slip shoes. With a few minimal precautions it is possible to be safe and devote your energies to seashore observations. Many people find that the favourite part of the holiday turns out to be that spent lying full length gazing into a pool, or knee-deep with a net hunting a velvet swimming crab.

Just like other habitats, though, the seashore needs conserving. It can easily suffer if too many people use it without consideration. Some of the most interesting shores are those normally within an army firing range, but made safe and opened for a short period. There, it may be possible to find enormous numbers of animals such as gaily coloured squat lobsters and young conger eels high on the shore. With care it is possible to observe and get a great deal of pleasure from the seashore without damaging the lives of its inhabitants.

As I write this I am off to the Isle of Mull in Scotland. I expect to have a marvellous time looking at seashore life there, and shall also be going inland, hoping to see golden eagles and other highland species. But, with the exception of the seashore, the total number of kinds of animals and plants present in this 'wild' part of Britain is far fewer than could be seen by any of us near to home in the habitats described in this book. Enjoy reading about what can be seen, then go out into your garden or park, go and explore your local ponds, note what grows on your roadsides. These places may be heavily influenced by man, but there is still an amazing variety of wildlife. Finally, on holiday, enjoy the fringes of the sea, where the land meets the least explored part of our planet.

JOHN STIDWORTHY

1
GARDEN AND PARK

Lying flat on the grass in the hot sunshine of a summer's day quickly brings about a dreamlike state of mind. The sun makes rainbow patterns in half-opened eyelashes and a pink glare burns through closed eyes. With the warmth making us lazily contented, our attention focuses on small sounds: the buzzing of insects; bird song; the hum of traffic. With minds pleasantly blank, we watch the sky, speculating on the movements of drifting clouds and watching the sun catch the wing of a high white seagull. In such receptive contact with Mother Earth, many of us feel closer to nature than at any other time.

Gardens and parks are our everyday contact with nature. It is noticeable that the greatest builders of them have been the urban cultures furthest removed from close contact with the countryside. They supply something we need that is otherwise absent from town life.

It is interesting to see how different types of garden reflect varying attitudes. The practical person exploits nature and grows vegetables; the sensitive grows flowers, shrubs and trees. Most suburban gardeners see nature as an unruly opponent and strive mightily to attain the smoothest of straight-edged lawns, waging ceaseless war on insects and 'weeds' in their tidy, sparsely stocked flowerbeds. They are really only a step away from adopting the 'final solution' of flagstones and plastic gnomes.

Whatever our feelings, though, nature remains undefeated. Even in the most barren of flagstone 'gardens' she holds outposts — a few mosses, a tenacious weed here and there, a few inevitable insects and birds. With their thousands of foreign and man-bred plant varieties, gardens and parks form the most varied habitat in Britain. As a result they provide opportunities for a surprising range of animal wildlife — and are the most easily accessible hunting-ground of all for the amateur naturalist.

Not that much hunting is required: the wildlife positively forces itself on us as we lie out in the sun or stroll around looking at our plants. Even if we can avoid noticing bird song we can never escape the insects. They land on us, crawl over us and attract the attention of the sleepiest sunbather with their mysterious comings and goings in the jungle of grass stems near his face.

Gardens and parks now represent a considerable proportion of the land that has not been built over. It has been calculated that private gardens alone make up a greater area than all the nature reserves in Britain. Many of their present wild inhabitants are species that have successfully adapted themselves from life in the forests as these have steadily been felled over the years. Much of our remaining woodland today consists of artificially planted conifers, lacking the variety that wildlife needs. Large areas of marshland have been drained; even the hedgerows that have provided refuges for animals and plants displaced from woodland are now being reduced. Modern agricultural techniques have changed plant populations and chemical poisons are spread by farmers in the countryside and by factories in towns.

Gardens and parks, most of which are in urban areas, are also subject to all the conditions of our new environment — but they have a few positive advantages to offer. In both summer and winter, the air temperature is a degree or two higher than out in the countryside; and there is less wind, because of the many buildings nearby. There may be slightly more rain, but it is drained away from the soil more rapidly. The diversity of environment and plant species is artificially high. Man has also become a reliable provider of food, willingly and unwillingly, to the many animal species able to take advantage of it.

Taking advantage is what spells success for animal opportunists in gardens and parks. Birds in particular have many success stories to tell us.

Birds

The blackbird (*Turdus merula*) is now Britain's commonest bird. It originally lived in the depths of the ancient forests, then occupied the hedgerows of the newer agricultural landscape. Only during the last century has it really made itself at home in towns and suburbs, yet already it is far commoner there than it is in the countryside.

Rural blackbirds are largely insect eaters and are commonly seen noisily turning over dried leaves in the undergrowth, in search of grubs and insects. They prefer to feed on the ground. In towns they eat a much higher proportion of vegetable matter, and this behaviour alone gives them an advantage over less broadminded birds.

Blackbirds are notoriously unparticular about their choice of nest site. Many fledglings become easy prey for cats because a nest has been built in a drainpipe or in an exposed wall, instead of deep in a nearby bush which seems far safer. It would be more realistic to call blackbirds 'adaptable' rather than 'stupid', however, as this very characteristic enables them to nest where fussier birds cannot.

Blackbirds in the countryside tend to move around a lot, especially in winter when food is scarce. Urban blackbirds seem to be a more settled population. Every winter large numbers of blackbirds migrate to Britain from the harsher conditions of northern Europe, but very few of these immigrants come near our gardens.

Blackbird (*Turdus merula*)

A particularly famous example of bird opportunism has been the remarkable way that great tits and blue tits have learned how to open milk bottles and steal milk. They made this discovery in the 1920s, when milk bottles were sealed with a disc of waxy cardboard; other tits learned by imitation and the habit

14

spread like wildfire. The introduction of metal foil bottle tops did not stop them for long.

How did the first tit find out that there was a rich source of food underneath? The answer is probably connected with the way tits commonly feed on insects by ripping pieces of loose bark from trees. They are so addicted to this habit that they were recorded in times past as notorious vandals in paper factories, flying in and ripping to shreds unattended sheets of damp, newly manufactured paper. Perhaps this behaviour has more than once revealed unsuspected food supplies to them.

Although often infuriating, it is impressive to see how these birds continue to defeat all sorts of counter-measures intended to protect milk on our doorsteps. The natural curiosity of tits has been their great asset in urban environments, although they have remained much more conservative than the blackbirds in their choice of food and nesting sites.

In any garden visited by tits it is quite easy to conduct all sorts of fascinating experiments to test their ability to exploit new sources of food. A simple one requires the construction of a device that rewards the bird with a peanut when it tugs away a matchstick. When the first tit has discovered this, which will usually not take long, you can watch other tits learning by imitation. Next, you can try making devices which require two, or even more, matchsticks to be removed before a peanut falls out.

Blue tit (*Parus caeruleus*)

House sparrows (*Passer domesticus*) are much more versatile than tits, and readier to fit into totally man-made environments. What is more, they are aggressive birds, operating in gangs. They have probably lived close to man ever since he began to cultivate grain, because they are basically seed eaters. Now they have become skilful all-rounders, feeding in the same ways as

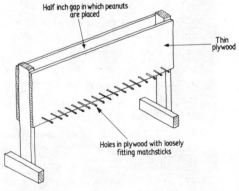

Half inch gap in which peanuts are placed

Thin plywood

Holes in plywood with loosely fitting matchsticks

Intelligence test for tits

15

any number of more specialised birds, including the tits. They are one of the very few bird species adaptable enough to thrive in our city centres.

No bird is more characteristic of cities than the pigeon (*Columba livia*). There is archaeological evidence that they have been reared by man for thousands of years, perhaps originally in the Middle East, in the past being an important source of food. Our city birds are feral pigeons, the descendants of these domesticated ones, constantly being joined by defecting racing pigeons and from time to time interbreeding with the wild rock doves of our coastal cliff-faces. These truly wild rock doves probably represent the ancestral stock from which the very first domestic pigeons were once taken. It is interesting to note how the nesting and roosting places of city pigeons are similar to sea cliffs, small ledges high above the traffic which rumbles below them like the sea. They are successful scavengers and thieves and are often deliberately fed. Totally at home in their new environment they have even been known to construct their untidy nests entirely with tangled pieces of wire.

Our wild, native woodpigeon (*Columba palumbus*), distinguished by its white neck patches, was first a shy forest-dweller, more recently coming out to plunder man's crops. Now it is a common sight in our parks, where it is strikingly bolder than its rural brethren which are extremely wary of man. It is not a very common visitor to most gardens, where the 'pigeon'

Woodpigeon (*Columba palumbus*)

usually seen is the collared dove (*Streptopelia decaocto*), which is rapidly colonising areas of suburban gardens all over Europe. From its original home in Northern India, it has spread outwards as it learned to exploit this new environment. Collared doves first reached Britain in 1955 and are still on the increase here. They are fawn-coloured, smaller than feral pigeons and with dark neck-markings.

Several species of seagulls, especially herring gulls and black-headed gulls, have become quite common well inland. This is largely as a result of the growth of gigantic rubbish dumps where they feed. Their populations are also on the increase. They are a familiar sight in our city parks, especially those with a lake. They do not come into gardens so much, partly because they seem to be timid of enclosed spaces. Some individuals overcome this fear, especially in coastal suburbs, where rooftops have been adopted as nesting-sites.

Yet another opportunist is the starling (*Sturnus vulgaris*), successful partly because it is bold and gregarious like the house-sparrow, another bird-table bully. They roost

18

together in large numbers at night outside the nesting season. A secluded patch of coniferous woodland may be selected, or often a group of tall, city-centre buildings. Watching them arrive is one of the marvels of nature. They fly in from all directions, often in smallish flocks of several hundred birds, merging into one gigantic flock that wheels and swerves to and fro in the sky like a single, shapeless monster. The purpose is probably to signal the location of the roost to the incoming flocks. When the main flock passes overhead, the sky darkens and there is literally a roar of wings. There is safety in numbers from predators, and roosts in city centres also offer a degree of warmth and shelter. The sheer numbers of roosting birds can produce problems, their droppings disfiguring buildings and often killing trees. I have crept up to the edge of a woodland starling roost after dark when the birds were settled, and found the smell utterly overpowering. A challenging project for someone with a car is to find out where the starlings in your area roost. Look out for the small flocks heading there in the evening and note their direction. You will not find the roost straight away, because they often travel a considerable distance.

Starlings visit gardens in much smaller bands and are charming birds, despite their bullying. They are expert mimics and can regularly be heard copying the calls of other birds, and even of cats.

A thriving population of waterfowl is often to be seen on lakes in city parks. Many are native British ducks, geese and swans, with a smattering of colourful foreign ducks and artificially bred forms. Although many of them are tame, full-time residents, a sizeable proportion are likely to be totally wild. This is a particularly moving example of opportunism, for there are few creatures more timid and wary of man than wild ducks on a marsh. They have been hunted by man for thousands of years. But each winter, as flocks of migrating wildfowl sweep across our skies, refugees from the bitter cold of Scandinavia and Russia, some of them are enticed down by the sight of our city park ducks and land amongst them. They quickly feel sufficiently reassured temporarily to lose their fear of man. Who is to say if the wigeon that gratefully accepts your crust of bread in St James' Park is a true-bred Londoner or a Russian defector? If he continues his journey a

Wigeon (*Anas penelope*)

British wildfowler might be shooting at him tomorrow.

These birds have successfully cashed in on the environmental changes caused by man. So have many other species, to a greater or lesser degree. All British birds have been forced to adapt to our presence and our gardens and parks are occasionally visited even by the more conservative species that still prefer to live in the old marsh and woodland habitats.

Everybody wants to have birds in their garden. They can be encouraged to come by providing both food and suitable nesting and roosting sites.

Seeds, fruits, worms and insects are the most important foods of garden birds. The easiest way to provide all these is to be a bad gardener. Just about everything the 'good' gardener prides himself on is bad for birds (and garden wildlife in general). For a start, he introduces into the garden all sorts of outlandish plants, originating from the four corners of the earth. The fact is that there is a lot more than meets the eye in the complex relationships between plants and insects (insects = bird food). In their native lands, those foreign plants with their attractive flowers are associated with all sorts of insect species, but not in Britain. Most of our native insects do not know what to make of them and their fruits and seeds are not always palatable to our birds. In contrast, our wild British plants are bread-and-butter to incredible numbers of insect species. These are the plants that will establish themselves, given half a chance: our much-persecuted 'weeds'. Many weeds are extremely beneficial to wildlife producing a rich crop of harmless insects to feed our birds. Nettles are particularly good.

It is easy to see this principle in operation. Sycamore trees are often planted because they are hardy and fast-growing. Nevertheless they are not a true British species. Walk through any sycamore wood and notice the comparative scarcity of bird life and the relatively small variety of insect species. Now walk through an oak wood and just see the difference. Oak trees have thrived in Britain since the time our ancestors were chipping out flint axe-heads and they are a paradise for insect-eating birds (to say nothing of those that eat the acorns).

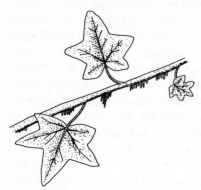

Ivy (*Hedera helix*)

Incidentally, ivy is another useful plant that does *not* harm a tree unless it actually manages to cut off the light from the tree's leaves, which it seldom does. It is also very attractive to insects and provides good nesting and roosting cover, as well as plenty of berries.

The 'good' gardener is also far too tidy. A compost heap is an excellent thing to have, but a proportion of the dead leaves and twigs should be left lying about. Hordes of tiny insects will obligingly help return the essential elements to the soil, and feed the birds at the same time. Larger pieces of dead wood should also be left to rot naturally, not rushed to the bonfire. They provide the insects with shelter as well as food. The tidy, bare soil of a weed-free flowerbed is far less hospitable to the small creatures which are benefiting the plants as well as the birds. This is partly because of the extremes of temperature that affect unprotected soil. A layer of compost on the surface helps here.

More will be said later about the terrible harm we have done to our bird life by the use of insecticide poisons. Too many of us see nature as an enemy to be defeated, reaching instinctively for the bottle or aerosol can of spray when we see something move in a flower. The true gardener should study to achieve a state of balance and harmony. Each of us is a small part of nature.

It is worth leaving at least a part of the garden to go wild, no matter how small. A few square metres will not provide enough to support a single bird, yet it will attract brief visits from many birds as they forage from garden to garden. The number of bird species noticed in your garden will probably increase as a result.

Feeding garden birds with scraps is not a thing to be undertaken lightly. It is not fair to stop once you have started, especially in winter, because additional birds will soon be attracted to your garden and there may no longer be enough food to go round if your offerings stop coming. In the winter, a bird that is positively overweight can starve to death within a single day, such a high proportion of its food is required to keep it warm.

The conventional bird table has a lot to commend it, but your own or your neighbours' cats can be a problem. The diagram below shows the simplest design. The post should be at least five feet high to lift the table beyond cat-pouncing range. Similarly, there should not be any cover below it, at ground level, that might allow an ambush. Even so, the bird table should not be too far from the nearest tree or shrub because many birds are timid about coming right out in the open.

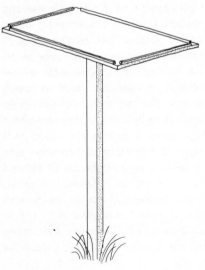

Simple bird table

21

The strips of wood round the edge of the table prevent food being blown or knocked off. A piece of wire netting bent to fit snugly over the table on top of the food is another possibility. Some birds, such as blackbirds, prefer to feed on the ground. Whether or not you should encourage this depends rather on the extent of the local cat problem.

If the table has a roof, the food will be kept dry and the shelter will be appreciated by the birds in bad weather. It will also permit the use of a seed hopper. Wild-bird seed is available from pet shops and it is mixed to suit a wide range of species. Once again, the supply must never run out once you have started, so a plastic seed hopper is the ideal solution. It must be sheltered from the rain or else the seed will swell and jam inside.

Garden birds should be offered a wide variety of foods. Almost any kitchen leftovers are suitable, but a diet of nothing but breadcrusts is as harmful to birds as it would be to us. Fat is especially valuable in the winter because it contains twice as much energy (for warmth) as any other food. A tit bell (not what I thought it was when I first heard of it) is a suspended bell-shaped container into which a warmed mixture of fat and various other delicacies such as seeds, grated cheese and cut-up bacon rinds can be poured and allowed to set; or you can use a half-coconut shell. Hang up the half-coconut with a piece of

thick galvanised wire first, so that the tits can clean it out before you pour in the fat mixture. In this way, tits are not forced to compete with various bullies on the bird table and their acrobatics are fun to watch.

Certain foods can be harmful to birds. These include dry foods such as desiccated coconut and uncooked rice, which are likely to swell up inside them. It is especially important to avoid giving these in the nesting season. Growing young fledglings especially need a balanced diet, with plenty of protein, and unless this can be guaranteed it is probably better to stop feeding birds at this time. There is plenty of natural food available by then and nobody would want to rear a human baby on breadcrusts.

Birds badly need water in dry summer weather and when it freezes in the winter. Once again, do not just give them some when you think about it but have a daily routine.

Tits are often persuaded to nest in gardens if suitable nestboxes are provided. It is an unfortunate fact that by encouraging this we are not always helping the birds. A far higher proportion of young tits die of starvation in gardens than out in the countryside. The problem is the shortage of insects and grubs which are essential to the young birds. Unless we have a good-sized country garden it may be best to let the birds seek out better nesting places for themselves. They will be back at the bird table soon enough.

Plants

Mention the word 'garden' and everybody thinks of flowers. Flowers represent such an attractive aspect of nature that it is small wonder that they have always been used by mankind for decorative purposes. Gardeners cultivate them in millions, even though most serve no other function. Our obsession with them can be seen in the way we use the word 'flower' when often we should say 'plant'. We frequently forget that a flower is just a relatively small part of a plant.

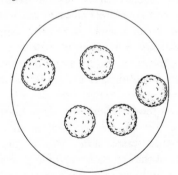

Pollen grains under the microscope

Of course, the purpose of the bright colours and strong perfumes is to attract insects, which assist the plant to reproduce by carrying pollen from flower to flower. Each yellowish, microscopic, dust-like pollen grain contains a full set of genetic 'designs' from the plant that produced it. If the pollen grain is fortunate enough to land on the female part of a flower, it sends out a thin tube which eventually penetrates one of the young, green, undeveloped seeds. This young seed also contains a set of genetic instructions from *its* parent plant. After fertilisation by the pollen grain, the seed ripens and if it can germinate it develops eventually into a young plant with some of the characteristics of each parent. This is a form of sexual reproduction. Flowers are sex organs.

Plants can also reproduce asexually, by a process requiring only one parent. In this way, various plants send out 'runners' or 'suckers', underground or above ground, each one terminating in a young plant. Bulbs divide underground, and the taking of plant cuttings is an artificial example of asexual reproduction. So why do plants bother with the much more complicated sexual process involving the hit-and-miss transfer of pollen?

The answer is important because it applies to all living creatures, both plants and animals. Evolution is the very slow process by which living things make sure that they are always well adapted to the environment they live in. Environments are always changing, so it is vital that plants and animals should be able to change as well, even though it may take millions of years. Evolution works by natural selection, only the best-designed plants and animals surviving to pass on their characteristics to the next generation. In this way, unsuitable features are 'weeded out' and the species becomes better and better adapted to its environment.

This natural selection depends on there being small differences between all the individual plants of a species so that slightly different designs can constantly be tried out. Sexual reproduction combines the characteristics of two parents, thereby greatly increasing the amount of variation between individual offspring. In doing this it helps evolution. Simple, asexual reproduction still has its place with many plants and even animals (such as garden aphids), largely because it can be such a rapid way of producing large numbers of offspring. However, there are few living organisms which do not reproduce sexually at least occasionally, in order to increase variation and so help evolution.

The earliest land plants, flourishing long before the first dinosaurs, had no flowers; the first insects were only just appearing and had not yet developed the power of flight. From that time onwards, insects and flowering plants have evolved together, many species of each becoming closely dependent on the other. The plants developed flowers to attract insects, because relying on wind to carry pollen had always been a wasteful process. Colourful petals appeared, impregnated with attractive scents and with patterns to guide the insect to the heart of the flower. Some of these patterns are only visible in ultra-violet light, so insects can see them but we cannot.

At first the insects fed on the pollen, which was acceptable to the plants because they still wasted less than the wind did, and they were in this way encouraged to transfer pollen from flower to flower on their hairy bodies. Later, flowers developed sweet, sticky nectar to reward and attract their insect friends. Try tasting some nectar. Break off the pointed end of the trumpet-shaped nasturtium flower and suck out the nectar. Delicious, but watch out for aphids. In their turn, many insects developed special mouthparts and came to rely more or less entirely on flowers for their food. There are few clearer examples of the fact that no living creature stands alone, that all are a part of the complex web of life. So are we, and we are finding that by interfering with one species we cause unexpected repercussions somewhere else.

Some flowering plants have gone back to the idea of using wind to carry their pollen. Such flowers are

The secretive harvestman, distinguished from spiders by the one-piece body with no waist

'Pests'' paradise — a well-stocked country vegetable garden, with delphiniums in the background (*John Beach/Wildlife Picture Agency*)

Green-veined white butterfly

Young caterpillars only a few days old set to work on the underside of a cabbage leaf

Large garden with plenty of shrub cover for birds (*John Beach/Wildlife Picture Agency*)

Leaf miners, the tiny caterpillar-like larvae of certain flies and moths, create these distinctive marks by tunnelling inside the skin of a leaf

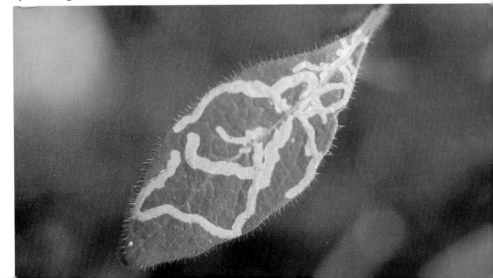

Lichen encrusting a stone — it will survive in the driest of places, but unpolluted air is essential. Lichens are seldom found near cities

Hoverfly basks on a Michaelmas daisy in autumn sunshine — such late flowering plants attract many other nectar feeders

normally small, lacking in colour and scent, and produce lots of pollen. Grass is an example. There are many species of grass, easily distinguished by the forms of the bushy flowers that appear wherever it is not trimmed back. The considerable amounts of grass pollen produced in high summer are a major cause of hay fever, many people being allergic to it.

Most flowers are insect-pollinated and their diversity is tremendous. A few are native British species, many others come from far-away countries. More still have been artificially bred by man, by a sort of controlled, accelerated form of evolution. The many forms of rose or tulip are two examples. Man, not natural selection, has chosen which of the varying individuals of each generation should be permitted to breed.

Despite the tremendous differences between species, the components shown in the diagram above can be seen in most flowers. The sepals are green scales outside, and sometimes protecting, the petals. The stamens manufacture pollen. The stigma (usually several) in the centre of the flower receives the pollen from another flower on its sticky surface. The pollen-tubes will then grow down to the young seeds in the ovary at its base. Nectar is produced in the nectaries at the base of the petals. Flowers of the dandelion and daisy family (*Compositae*) do not seem to fit this scheme, at first glance. In fact, each 'petal' and each 'bit' of the central part is actually a separate flower.

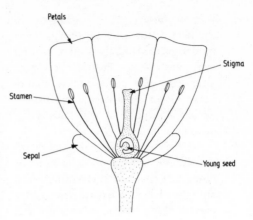

Parts of a flower

Daisy (*Bellis perennis*)

In some flowers there may be no sign of a stigma, and others may have no stamens. Such flowers are all-male pollen producers or all-female seed producers, but these are a minority. Most are bisexual. Generally the problem is to prevent self-pollination, because this will not produce as much of the vital variation between offspring. The usual way for this to be avoided is for the female part of each flower not to ripen until the stamens have withered away. In this way they can only be fertilised by pollen from

29

another flower. It is fascinating to examine a flower closely to see how its design deliberately coats a visiting insect with pollen. Push the bee-sized, blunt end of a pencil into a mature gorse flower for instance, and see the explosion of pollen as the stamens pop out.

Pressed flowers can make a particularly attractive collection or display. If each one is carefully spread out, then left on a flat surface under a pile of heavy books, it will dry out and keep its colour. Remove it after a couple of weeks. It will tend to stick to ordinary paper, but not to absorbent paper such as blotting or newspaper. Each flower can be sandwiched between the paper it is to be displayed on and another piece of newspaper. Alternatively, it can be sandwiched between two sheets of newspaper: it will not stick to either and can be mounted afterwards.

A collection of pressed grasses is equally interesting. Another way to preserve grasses is to dry them in tied bunches with the flower heads hanging upside-down. This way they dry straight and can be displayed in a vase.

Weeds

There is a very clear dividing line in the mind of the average gardener between 'flowers' and 'weeds'. Basically, it seems, a 'flower' is a plant honestly purchased with good money, or carefully propagated from a friend's plant and lovingly tended. A 'weed' is a plant that sneaked in by itself. It did not originate in a seed-packet, it has no label tied to it and it was not presented by a friend. Weeds have to be exterminated. In this context, their presence is probably good for the mental health of the gardener: the act of tearing them from the ground is a harmless enough channel for releasing aggression and all sorts of gardening ills and misfortunes can be blamed upon them.

However, there is no scientific basis for this distinction. The Oxford ragwort (*Senecio squalidus*) with its attractive yellow flowers originally lived on the slopes of volcanoes in Sicily. Some time ago it was a prized specimen in the Botanic Garden at Oxford. Presumably the effort

Annual meadow-grass (*Poa annua*)

expended in obtaining the first specimens qualified it as a 'flower'. Since then, it has spread everywhere in disturbed ground resembling its original home: building sites, railway lines and roadsides. What else is it now but a 'weed'?

Many of these plants are opportunists in rather a similar sense to those bird species described. Their main assets are often an ability to spread their seeds widely, perhaps on the wind, and sometimes the ability to survive where man has disturbed the soil, or burnt it, or altered its chemical nature. This is where certain weeds have the greatest advantage over other plants, whereas in normal conditions they may not be able to compete with them.

Plants do compete. Although the resources they compete for are few enough (light, dissolved elements and sometimes water), any innocent-looking group of plants is involved in a vicious, no-holds-barred struggle for existence. The idea is to grow faster than your neighbour, reach out your leaves above him and take all the light, spread out your roots and take all the available dissolved elements; certain unscrupulous species, including the cucumber, are even suspected of poisoning their neighbours.

If you are no good at such hand-to-hand combat, as many weeds are not, why not just cash in on being the first to arrive in any new environment? When some ground is newly dug over, make sure your abundant seeds get there first and establish yourself

before your rivals. They will come and take over before long, but by then a fresh load of your seeds will have been spread abroad. If at the same time you can tolerate conditions that other plants cannot, so much the better.

Dandelions (*Taraxacum offininale*), groundsel (*Senecio vulgaris*), thistles (*Cirsium spp.*) and the tall, purple spikes of rosebay willowherb (*Epilobium angustifolium*), can all be weeds of this type. At a later stage, nettles (*Urtica dioica*) and brambles (*Rubus fruticosus*) are likely to establish themselves. Their presence is often an indication that the ground has been disturbed. Eventually, shrubs and trees will rise above them, if given the time. All this represents a natural succession, leading towards Britain's

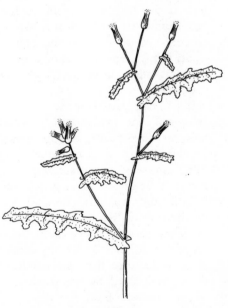

Groundsel (*Senecio vulgaris*)

31

natural 'climax community', which is woodland.

Just how harmful are weeds to the plants we really try to grow in the garden? We usually have definite ideas on the plants we want, and do not choose to leave the various combatants to fight it out according, literally, to the law of the jungle. For this reason some weeding is essential. But once the desired flowers or vegetables have become established, is it really necessary to follow a scorched-earth policy by trying to eliminate weeds entirely?

It is certainly not a natural state of affairs for naked soil to remain indecently exposed for any length of time. A mat of plant cover will protect it from burning heat in summer and frost in the winter, to the probable benefit of the essential microscopic life in the soil. A far better substitute for weeds is to sow a selection of low, ground-hugging plants in any empty spaces, or at least to cover the soil with a layer of compost.

It is true that the weeds are competing for raw materials with more treasured plants, but the worst possible thing to do is continually to tidy them away to a distant heap in a corner of the garden. It is not quite so bad if the resulting compost is regularly re-applied to the soil, but many people are not conscientious about this. All they are actually doing is to make sure that the essential elements absorbed by the weeds are totally removed from the reach of other plants. If a low cover of weeds is

regularly cut back with shears and the cuttings left to decompose, a state of equilibrium is reached, with elements being returned to the soil as fast as they are taken out. Under those conditions, weeds are only actually competing with other plants during the time they are establishing themselves on bare soil, and even that competition may not be considerable.

There are other benefits from this policy. Those most hated of weeds, the ones with roots that penetrate deep into the ground are taking in dissolved elements from a level well below the reach of most other plants. When they die back, they do the soil an inestimable service by enriching its surface layers with those same elements. Certain plants can assist the growth of others in different ways that are hard to understand. It is generally known that plants of the pea family have bacteria associated with their roots that take nitrogen from the air and store it in the soil. That is straightforward enough, but any old-fashioned gardener also knows of all sorts of planting combinations that seem to benefit the plants concerned, though we cannot explain them and they are not mentioned in most gardening books.

There is evidence, for instance that surrounding nettles give increased yields of tomatoes, so possibly other weeds may also have such beneficial effects, Experiments have shown that cabbages with a certain amount of weed growth around them suffer less from the attentions of caterpillars. Here we do know the reason: some species of beetle which prey on the caterpillars need the nearby cover from which to emerge to make their attacks at night, being themselves afraid of birds. The entry of a serious pest of country gardens, rabbits, is said to be discouraged by suitably positioned beds of wild foxgloves — but I have not tried this!

British wild flowers are having a rough time nowadays, and our gardens and parks have come to represent an important habitat for many of them. It is a pity we are so hard on them: perhaps we ought to stop using the word 'weeds'. These are the plants that attract most butterflies into our gardens, and produce seeds and support all sorts of insects to feed the birds.

The use of 'weed-killers' or herbicides should always be avoided. Those that work by interfering with a plant's growth hormones are probably very specific and relatively harmless, as the suppliers claim. Nevertheless, nobody can reliably forecast the full effects of adding any chemical to a living environment such as soil, which positively seethes with the interactions of an incredibly complex web of life. Lawn moss-killers for instance, often contain heavy doses of mercury, one of the nastiest and most persistent of cumulative poisons; people can absorb it directly or via fruit and vegetables.

Simple plants

Only the largest and most complex plants produce flowers. All sorts of simpler plants grow in a garden:

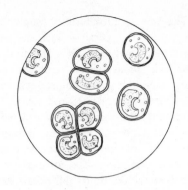

Tree-trunk algae under the microscope

instead of using flowers and seeds, most of them reproduce by means of tiny, windblown spores.

A green stain will be seen on any wall, fence, tree trunk, post or concrete gnome that is shaded from the full heat of the sun and so remains permanently damp. Often the growth is thick enough to rub off as a powder on skin or clothes. If a sample of this powder is examined under a microscope, it is seen to consist of tiny, green, rounded plant cells. This plant is one of the few algae that lives out of water. Various other types of algae may be found in areas that are permanently wet, rather than just damp — as described in the *Ponds and Streams* booklet in this series.

The possession of green chlorophyll is sufficient proof that this 'stain' is really a collection of tiny plants. Lacking a root system, it obtains water from the damp surface on which it lives. The small quantities of essential elements are dissolved partly from the damp surface and partly from dust settling on it. It obtains carbon dioxide from air, like other plants.

33

The most familiar form of fungus is the group of species which forms mushrooms and toadstools and those plate-like 'brackets' on tree trunks. Fungi lack the green chlorophyll so characteristic of plants, and for this reason they are sometimes considered to belong to a different group altogether, neither plant nor animal — not that they are affected by whatever we decide to call them. As they have no chlorophyll they cannot make their own food from sunlight, as the green plants do. For this reason fungi feed on decaying plant and animal material. There is plenty of this in the soil, and fungi are abundant there, usually unsuspected despite the important contribution they make towards the releasing of essential dissolved minerals from rotting plants.

Forgetting the familiar image of toadstools for a moment, a typical fungus is actually a tangled mass of tiny, branching threads. The whitish, cottonwool growths sometimes seen on 'mouldy' bread or fruit are a perfect example. The amazing thing is that mushrooms and toadstools are not individual plants. They simply represent places where the cottonwool growths that are everywhere in the soil below the lawn have grown together and burst out above the surface. It is as if the toadstools were all joined by the same root system.

The function of the toadstool part of the fungus is the spreading of the tiny reproductive spores typical of many simple plants. One reason for the umbrella shape is obvious enough: the spores must be kept dry, so that the wind will spread them better.

'Fairy rings' on the grass are simply giant underground versions of the little circular patches of fungus you may see on a mouldy piece of bread. The spore-bearing toadstools come up around the edge of the patch. The grass often grows much taller and greener inside the ring, showing how effectively fungi can release dissolved elements into the soil.

Lichens (usually pronounced 'likens', but take your pick) are brittle, scaly growths, often brightly coloured, on walls and tree trunks. They are extremely sensitive to air pollution by dust and chemicals and are a rare sight anywhere near cities or big towns. In such places the powdery green growths of algae seem far more common. There is no need to confuse the two — lichen, even when green, does not rub off on your finger.

As with insects and flowers, lichens provide a striking example of the way two totally different types of organism can become dependent on one another. Each patch of lichen consists of a fungus living in intimate contact with thousands of cells of algae, similar to the type found on tree trunks. Both members of this remarkable association benefit from it, because lichens thrive in relatively dry, sunny locations unsuitable either for algae or fungi on their own.

Mosses, ferns and horsetails are slightly more complex plants, but they still reproduce by spores rather than by flowers and seeds. They have come down in the world since the

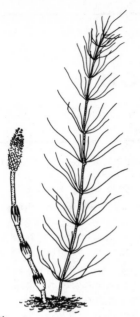

Horsetail

The hart's tongue fern so common on banks and walls in southern and western Britain, (*Phyllitis scolopendrium*) has undivided, strap-like fronds. But they all produce their spores in dark-coloured areas on the underside of each frond, and this readily distinguishes them from flowering plants.

Mosses are attractive plants when looked at closely. The wall screw-moss (*Tortula muralis*) is very common, as its name suggests, on walls and other man-made structures including paths and roofs. Its firm, velvety clumps send up numerous reddish spore cases on stalks.

These simple plants often play an important part in the plant succession that can colonise the barest of surfaces such as a flat roof. First a coating of algae or lichen appears, scorning the use of soil. As time passes, wind-blown dust and grit is trapped amongst these first plant growths, which respond by continuing to grow on top of the accumulating sediment. Dead remains of the algae decompose and begin to turn the grit into something resembling a soil. At this stage mosses are likely to appear, helping to stabilise the accumulating soil and adding their own remains to it. With the trapping of even more windblown grit, it is not long before conditions become suitable for flowering plants: perhaps grasses are the first to arrive.

This is the way our motorways may some day return to nature.

time when, hundreds of millions of years ago, as the first amphibians were crawling from the swamps, their ancestors towered up as gigantic trees. They were reduced to their present lowly status when the flowering, seed-producing plants evolved. They reproduce alternately with asexual spores and with tiny male 'sperms' that must have a damp surface in order to swim to a female 'egg'. For this reason, mosses, ferns and horsetails are only found in damp habitats.

Horsetails have fleshy stems that break easily in segments. From each 'joint' in the stem grows a whorl of rodlike leaves. The spores are raised up high in a special stalked container.

Ferns are not always fern-shaped.

In the soil

Soil is alive. Not only does it give life to the familiar plants we see, but also to teeming hordes of tiny plants and animals, some of which can only be seen with the aid of a microscope. Without these inhabitants soil would be a totally different substance, unable to grow most of our garden plants.

This underground world begins in the vegetation covering the soil's surface: in the case of the lawn, directly beneath our feet. Small insects are particularly common here, and from their viewpoint it is a dense jungle. We have already mentioned the example of the sleepy sunbather becoming involved with the progress of a small beetle through the maze of grass stems. Deeper in the turf, other creatures force their way among the roots, while deeper still there is a whole population of smaller animals living between the very soil particles themselves.

Just what is so important about these inhabitants of the soil?

Any self-sufficient animal community relies on plants for food. There may be some meat-eaters that attack smaller animals, but even they are linked to a food-chain that begins with plants being eaten by animals. The soil community is no exception, and in this case the plants growing on the surface represent the food source, mainly the dead plants or dead parts of plants like leaves and twigs. Anyone can see that these do not lie about on the ground for ever. They rot away quite quickly. There is nothing magical about this rotting process: it is simply that the inhabitants of the soil are feasting on the dead material. Many of the organisms responsible for the vital job of rotting, such as bacteria and fungi, are invisible to the naked eye, but if they were not there the dead plants simply would not decay. It is hard to imagine the rubbish disposal problem this would create for the average garden, but there is an even more important aspect.

As we have seen, unlike all animals, plants do not 'feed' in the normally accepted sense. They are unique in being able to make their own food by means of chlorophyll, that wonderful green substance in their leaves. Chlorophyll traps the energy of sunlight and uses it to power a living chemical factory geared to the production of all the necessary plant-building substances. Apart from light, all the plants need in the way of 'food' are carbon-dioxide gas from the air and, from the soil, water containing very small amounts of a definite range of dissolved elements such as nitrogen, phosphorus, calcium and many others.

The carbon dioxide and the water are seldom scarce, but certain of the minerals can be, even though only tiny traces are necessary. If only one essential element is lacking, plant growth can be seriously hindered or even prevented. In a healthy soil, the vital elements are released by the rotting of dead plant material as fast as the living plants are using them up. This is where the tiny underground inhabitants of the soil that cause decay are absolutely vital. It is such a complex and delicate balance, that it is possible that they also assist plant growth in other ways that we cannot even guess at. There is much to be said in support of the arguments against widespread use of pesticides and even chemical fertilisers. These substances can harm certain of the soil's inhabitants and might tend to upset the balance.

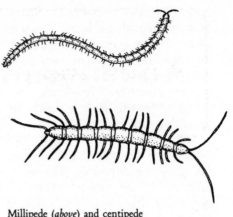

Millipede (*above*) and centipede

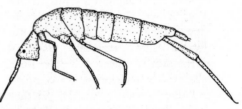

Springtail

The bigger soil animals

The simplest way to examine the non-microscopic soil animals is to spread out a large sheet of pale-coloured paper and dump a load of soil in the middle of it. It is not necessary to wait long in order to see what hops, scuttles, crawls, or wriggles out of it . Worms and beetles need no description. Centipedes are long, wriggly and fast-moving; they normally have less than the famous hundred legs and are carnivores, feeding on smaller animals. Millipedes are more tubular in shape, have shorter legs — and two pairs per segment as opposed to the centipede's one — and move slowly. Vegetarians, they travel around in 'bottom gear', numerous short legs bulldozing a pathway through all obstacles.

Small snails, slugs, spiders, woodlice and the grubs of a range of adult insects will also be more or less familiar. Anything smaller might well not be recognised. Springtails will certainly be noticed quickly. These tiny insects have a little spike on their

37

behind which is normally folded forwards beneath the body. When it clicks straight again the springtail is catapulted high in the air. The trick must have developed to enable it to escape predators. Bristletails are elongated insects with a couple of long, thin hairs trailing behind them.

Any creature with eight legs belongs to the spider and scorpion family — the Arachnids. The really tiny ones are mites, not all carnivorous like their larger cousins. Many mites are important decomposers. Some really tiny worms may be seen, perhaps a few millimetres long, whose bodies are not divided into segments like an earthworm's; these are nematode worms. They are extremely common and there are many species, yet they are so hard to identify, with their featureless bodies, that very little is known about them.

There is a simple and much more effective way of extracting these small creatures from the soil. It relies on their habit of moving downwards whenever the surface of the soil becomes too warm and dry for their liking. A cylinder is made from the largest tin can available, by cutting out both top and bottom. Certain large beer cans are very suitable. A piece of muslin is stretched tightly across one end and secured with a few turns of tape. The contraption is filled with soil from the garden which will be full of tiny creatures. The can is then rested on a cardboard funnel over a jam jar. Heat from a suitably arranged light bulb above drives all sorts of small animals downwards, only to fall, via the funnel, into the jar.

Earthworms are vitally important in a healthy garden. Not only do they feed on dead plant material: some species pull dead leaves down into their burrows, so speeding their decay by smaller organisms in the soil. Such leaves stand on end and can be quite conspicuous. Swallowed soil which has passed through their bodies is voided at the surface as 'worm casts'. This process also causes the gradual burial of plant material and mixes the soil. To top it all, these useful animals honeycomb the soil with a network of burrows which bring air to the plant roots and prevent waterlogging by draining away surplus water.

Earthworms are extremely numerous. In some agricultural areas they may even exceed the weight of farm livestock above ground. Small wonder that experiments have recently been conducted to investigate the possibility of making earthworms into human food. The amount of soil they bring up as worm casts is considerable: up to ten tons per acre per year, in fertile soil. Archaeologists owe a lot to earthworms because they are responsible for the burial of all sorts of objects. It is possible to estimate how many years earthworms would take to bury, say, a teacup left standing on a lawn.

With four wooden pegs and a length of string, mark out on the lawn a square with each side five metres long (250,000 square centimetres in area). Carefully remove all the worm casts within the square. One week later, collect all the casts which have appeared during the previous seven days. Measure their volume in millilitres (cubic centimetres). Divide that volume by 250,000 and the extremely small number you now have is the distance in centimetres that earthworms have raised the level of the lawn in one week, relative to the base of our imaginary disappearing teacup. If you are not impressed, try multiplying your figure by 5,200 to discover the height, in centimetres, of an object they could bury in a century. Bear in mind that earthworms are much more active in the summer, as you do the experiment and interpret the results.

An earthworm's body is filled with water and its muscles act by squeezing against this water. When the muscles that run round the worm squeeze, the worm gets long and thin. When the muscles that are arranged lengthways along the body shorten, the worm gets short and fat. Inside, the worm is divided into a series of separate watertight compartments, so that one part can be long and thin at the same time as another is short and fat. Small bristles also help the worm grip the sides of its burrow as it pushes forward.

Worms are often accidentally cut in half while the garden is being dug. The front end will survive, provided that the head and the 'saddle' containing the reproductive organs are intact. The doomed rear end nobly acts as a decoy, wriggling and thrashing while the front creeps stealthily away.

When digging during dry weather in the summer you often find worms tangled up in a motionless, slimy knot. This is a temporary response to unfavourably dry conditions; worms may simply curl up and go to sleep for a few weeks until the soil becomes moist again.

Insects

Most people do not like insects — except perhaps butterflies. The natural history of a garden, many would think, should deal with flowers, birds and small mammals, perhaps with a quick, brave look at toads and earthworms. Book dealers and publishers know that books on insects do not sell all that well.

To be widely popular with people, an animal has to have some human-type characteristics. Better still, it should have resemblances to a human infant, in order to trigger off our powerful protective instincts. It should be warm and soft, with a rounded outline, melting eyes and attractive face. The koala bear heads the list of course (but is none too common in our gardens); cats and dogs, squirrels, birds (especially owls), hedgehogs, fieldmice — all these are acceptable to most of us.

The list of disliked creatures is just as revealing. We forgive the owl its eerie calls in the night because of its round body and human face; no such pardon for rats and bats if they startle us in the dark. Our other instinctive dislikes are for those often faceless creatures impossible to compare with a cuddly baby: insects, spiders, snakes, centipedes, slugs, worms . . .

Insects are not warm but cold; not soft but hard and shiny; not rounded but jointed; their jewelled compound eyes are far from human. These unfortunate animals receive no mercy from us; their feelings must be so alien to ours that we shrink from contemplating them. Nevertheless we cannot ignore the insects.

For a start, the number of insects in a garden can be greater than the number of people in Britain. But that is not all. The insects are a very successful group even if success is measured by the number of species rather than the number of individuals. If we look, we can find more insect species in our gardens than all other species of animals and plants put together. The sheer number of species is in fact a scientists' nightmare.

It would not be difficult to discover a totally new insect species in an average garden. Your problem would be to find out which is a new species, because no single reference book contains more than a fraction of the 20,000-odd so far recorded in Britain. How many could you identify? I have yet to identify a gigantic, pure yellow swallow-tailed butterfly that appeared in my garden some years ago. I am no expert on butterflies, but I have established that it was not a native British species.

Insects are immensely strong. Their skeleton is not internal like ours but is worn outside, like a suit of armour. This gives their muscles much more leverage. Periodically, however, they have to shed their armour in order to grow. Because of the inconvenience of this, many insects have evolved the system of having a larval (or grub) stage; the young larva's main job is to feed and grow. It then forms an intermediate pupa, or chrysalis, from which the adult insect later emerges. Most of the more familiar insects develop in this way, and then the adults do not need to grow. Their main task is to mate and lay eggs.

All insects have six legs, a fact sufficient to distinguish them from other animals such as spiders, woodlice and centipedes, which also possess rather similar 'outside skeletons'. Insects' bodies are divided into three parts — head, thorax and abdomen. Most of them possess compound eyes which are made up of numerous lenses, each forming a separate image; no human can hope to imagine what an insect sees. Such is the basic plan of an insect and the variations on that theme appear to be almost infinite.

Of the many insect groups, perhaps the flies are the ones we notice first. Their distinguishing feature is the possession of one pair of wings. (Some

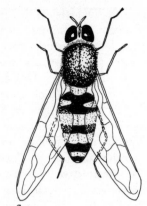

Hoverfly

insects have two pairs, others have none.) The various species of hoverflies are charming examples and can be seen in almost any garden, any summer's day. They hover in the sunshine, remaining motionless, then darting rapidly to a fresh position. Despite this distinctive characteristic, hoverflies are generally mistaken for wasps because of their banded yellow-and-black bodies. In fact they are perfectly harmless and feed on nectar. Their coloration is a cunning plot to fool birds into thinking they are stinging wasps, so that they will be left alone. The caterpillar-shaped larvae of some hoverfly species feed on aphid pests like the greenfly. Other species have larvae that live in beehives or wasps' nests and are tolerated by the inhabitants because they act as useful scavengers.

There are so many types of fly that it is hard to select examples. Bluebottles (*Calliphora vomitoria*) and houseflies (*Musca domestica*) or similar species will often be seen, perhaps basking in the sunshine on a wall.

Their larvae are the maggots that feed on dead animals. Mosquitoes develop as wriggling larvae in small areas of standing water and the females bite us for a taste of our blood before egg-laying. They produce a high pitched hum as they fly past, because they flap their wings at the incredible rate of 500 times per second. The large, long-legged daddy-long-legs (*Tipula oleracea*) has a destructive larva known as the leatherjacket, which leads a hell's angel's life in the soil, vandalising plant roots.

Some time ago, when a distinguished biologist was asked what his lifetime's study of nature had demonstrated to him about the Mind of the Creator, he replied, 'An inordinate fondness for beetles.' He had a point. The colossal number of insect species has already been emphasised, yet there are more species in the beetle group than in the rest put together. Beetles are distinguished by their front pair of wings which have become a tough protective shell for the hind pair. The hind wings can be unfolded for flight if necessary.

The attractive ladybird is surely the most familiar beetle of all. There are several ladybird species, sporting various numbers of spots, and not all of them are red. The common two-spotted ladybird (*Coccinella bipunctata*) sometimes has more than two spots and the colours are occasionally reversed — to, black with red spots. Ladybirds deserve our affection because they and their larvae, in company with the hoverfly larvae, are great eaters of aphids.

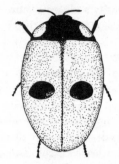

Two-spotted ladybird (*Coccinella bipunctata*)

Other carnivorous beetles attack such garden nuisances as caterpillars, while many beetles assist us by feeding on decomposing wood and plant remains. Others, such as the 'weevils' of which there are more species than any other beetle, are plant-eaters. Weevils have a long snout, reminiscent of an elephant's trunk.

The aphids, or greenfly, are very familiar garden pests. They are tiny, fragile looking insects, with fat bodies and flimsy legs. Most have no wings, but winged forms develop from time to time. Not all aphids are green; black ones ('blackfly') are often seen

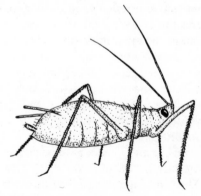

Aphid

42

on beans, for example. Other species are brown, grey or reddish.

Aphids feed by sucking the sugary sap from plants. They have to swallow a lot of sugar in order to obtain enough essential protein. As a result they get rid of much surplus sugar in the form of drops of sticky 'honeydew', which ants love to eat. Any motorist parking his car under an aphid-infested tree in the summer soon finds it covered with tiny sticky droplets. Lime trees are especially prone to this.

Nearly all aphids are females, and are able to reproduce without mating. As mentioned earlier, the big advantage of such 'asexual' reproduction is that it builds up big populations very quickly. This is the secret of the success of aphids. The young are born alive, with no eggs, and they themselves begin to produce offspring within days. The population explosion on a plant under attack can seem like magic. These are all female aphids.

Every now and again, a few winged female aphids are born. These fly off to start new colonies on other plants. At the end of the summer, winged males are also produced, and, after mating and egglaying, the fertilised eggs survive the hardships of winter, ready to hatch out the following spring. So aphids also have the advantages of some sexual reproduction.

Patches of white foam are often noticed on plant stems in the summer; they are commonly called 'cuckoo-spit' because they appear around the time that the first cuckoos arrive, but the foam is produced by the young nymph of the froghopper. These insects feed by sucking water from the veins of the plant stem. They have to swallow a lot of it in order to obtain enough dissolved food substances, and the excess water is whipped to a froth by the young insect's tail. The foam provides it with shelter and keeps it moist. Adult froghoppers are about a quarter of an inch long and are rather frog-shaped. They leap a long way when disturbed, usually out of sight. The commonest froghopper (*Philaenus spumarius*) is the one that produces the familiar cuckoo-spit.

Grasshoppers and crickets are familiar to most people. They are often heard more than they are seen, especially on sunny days when their chirping seems to fill the air in any

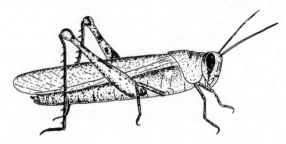

Grasshopper

area of long grass. The sound is made by the males, some species rubbing their wings together, others rubbing their wings and hind legs. There are many species, some vegetarian, some eating other insects. Generally, crickets can be distinguished from grasshoppers by having two or more 'tails' at the end of the abdomen. These probably detect air movements and sounds. Apart from the mole cricket which burrows, these insects rely on leaping to escape danger and many have lost the ability to fly.

Unlike most insects, grasshoppers and crickets do not have young grub-like 'larvae' that look different from the adults. Their 'nymphs' are smaller, wingless versions of the adults and have to moult periodically as they grow. Other insect groups that develop in this way are aphids, froghoppers and earwigs, to name a few.

Earwigs are much maligned but probably do little harm in the average garden. They will eat almost anything and may commit the crime of taking an occasional nibble at the petals of a prized flower. Probably their main crime lies in being insects. They have a pair of wings folded away, but seldom use them. Those fearsome-looking pincers at the rear end seem to be used for packing away the wings under the wing-cases, not for nipping human beings or anything else. They delight in hiding away in dark crevices and emerge to feed at night. They are one of the few insect groups that look after their young after they hatch out.

Solitary wasp

Ants, bees and wasps all belong to the same insect group. Different species have developed varying degrees of social harmony; they are masters of politics.

Most species of wasps and bees are capitalists, with a strong belief in private enterprise. These species are less familiar to most people, and do not live in groups but are solitary, each female laying a brood of eggs on her own. The solitary wasps are not yellow-banded like their social cousins, but can be recognised by their elongated bodies and extremely narrow waists. Many lay their eggs in a burrow and leave a store of paralysed insects or grubs for their young to feed on when they hatch. The free-living, solitary bees are also less generally familiar. They too lay their eggs in private, but their larvae are more vegetarian than wasps'. Again there are many species, not to be confused with the social bees, which are not capitalists.

At the other end of the political

scale, all the ants are communists. The 'state', or ant colony, comes first, and the only value of the individual lies in the service it can offer. Ants make no empty speeches about equality: they practise it. There are no privileges for anyone. The queens are egglayers and also serve as bureaucrats, regulating the activities of the underground colony. Yet any surplus queens must expect to be slaughtered ruthlessly by the workers. Those same workers will lay down their lives without hesitation in defence of the colony. There is nothing but endless toil, and death for any individual committing the unthinkable crime of arguing with the 'state'. There are no true leaders, not even the 'queens'. Each colony is ruled by the same set of instincts which is implanted in the minds of all its inhabitants.

In this sense, the ants differ from humans claiming to practise communism. We do not have those inborn, controlling instincts and so a human communist state needs human leadership. Also, our instincts are largely geared to self-preservation, and this can never be repressed without causing human suffering. If we really wished to live together in large units as efficiently as ants do, we would have to abandon the ideal of individual freedom. The only insects that are 'free' in this way are the solitary species. Mankind gave up a solitary existence with the coming of civilisation — so perhaps this is the political quandary that now faces us.

Ant-watching is an utterly absorbing pastime, as most young

Ant

children know. They prefer to build their underground colonies in sunny, well-drained pieces of ground. The black garden ant (*Acanthomyops nigra*) is the most familiar species. A sun-warmed garden path is the place to look for the workers, which are seen in two sizes, mostly one-eighth of an inch in length, with some of a quarter-inch. Foraging workers make frequent contact with each other's feelers, passing on the mysterious chemicals by which they communicate and coordinate their activities. Ants live in a world of smells and can easily be seen following winding, invisible 'smell trails' laid down by individuals finding a source of food. Place a half-sucked sweet on the path and watch this happen.

There are many intermediate degrees of 'civilisation' between the solitary insects and the ants. Social wasps and the handsome, wide-bodied bumble bees live in smallish colonies and the workers differ only in being smaller than the egg-laying queens. Bumble bees and some wasps (*Vespa vulgaris*) nest in burrows, while other wasps make papery nests in trees and shrubs. Bumble bees feed on nectar and pollen. Wasps are very fond of nectar and sweet, ripe fruit, but they

45

also devour vast numbers of insects, many of them garden pests. Wasp grubs eat only insects. Wasps are therefore useful in the garden and should not be destroyed; they never deliberately attack unless their nest is being threatened.

Honey bees (*Apis mellifera*) live in much larger groups with a more complicated social structure than bumble bees. They have been domesticated by man since prehistoric times. The worker bees gathering pollen and nectar from garden flowers are all females which are unable to reproduce. Tens of thousands of flowers must be visited in order to produce a single spoonful of honey, which is stored in the hive as a food reserve. Honey bees are also unwilling to sting unless greatly provoked; the barbed sting is torn from their body when used, and the bee dies shortly afterwards.

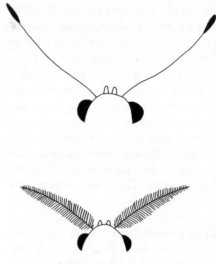

Antennae of the butterfly (*above*) and moth

Honey bee (*Apis mellifera*)

Butterflies and moths are an asset to the beauty of any garden. As in the ladybird, the bright colours of some species are partly an advertisement to hungry birds that the insect is not nice to eat. Usually, once a bird has

tasted one it will not take any more. The colours are produced by the unique little scales that cover the wings, and will rub off freely when the insect is handled. More subdued colours are usually visible when the wings are closed, better suited to camouflage. The larvae of butterflies and moths are mostly the grubs we call caterpillars.

The simplest way to tell a butterfly from a moth is to look at the antennae ('feelers'). Those of a butterfly have distinct knobs on the end, while those of a moth are more feathery and lack knobs. Moths tend to fold their wings flat down their backs, in contrast to butterflies. Butterflies fly by day and most moths are active at night. The pupa inside which the adult butterfly develops is usually angular and pointed and is attached to some vertical support like a wall or tree trunk. The pupa of a moth is more

46

rounded, wrapped in a silky cocoon and hidden away, often underground.

The caterpillar is a 'feeding machine', whose sole aim is to grow as fast as possible. Its metamorphosis inside the case of the pupa into a butterfly or moth is an often-quoted marvel; most other insects do much the same thing — and it really is a marvel. On forming the hard-shelled, nearly motionless pupa, all the various parts of the body literally dissolve into

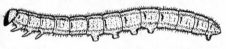

Caterpillar

a liquid soup. Within this gooey mass, a new body organises itself along totally different lines. Some time later, perhaps after waiting for the whole duration of the winter, the adult insect emerges, to dry its newly expanded wings in the sunshine.

It is easy to keep caterpillars in order to watch this transformation, but it is essential to give them the right plant to feed on. Each species has its own requirements and, if you cannot see what the caterpillar is eating when you collect it, the answer can be found in reference books. Gardens with plenty of 'weeds' or wild flowers have most butterflies.

Adult butterflies and moths feed on nectar from flowers, sucking it up through a long, tubular, rolled-up 'tongue' or proboscis. Some adult moths have no functioning mouthparts and survive only long enough to mate and lay eggs.

Goodies and baddies

A symptom of our increasing separation from nature is our tendency to classify wildlife according to whether it is helpful or harmful to our own immediate interests. Such an outlook is, of course, totally impractical: life is never that simple. Animals which tend to be harmful in one way often turn out to be indispensable allies in another. What is more, we are too quick to add to the 'baddies' list all those creatures whose appearance we dislike.

For millions of years, plants have coexisted with great hordes of small animals that feed on them. Anyone trying to stop this completely is taking on a direct confrontation with nature and is ultimately certain to cause major trouble in one way or another.

Garden plants are at greater risk of attack by various 'pests' than wild plants, for several reasons. For one thing, our tidy minds often direct us to grow our vegetables in large patches of one plant species only, free from weeds, flowers and other vegetables. This is a pests' paradise: abundant food, and ample opportunity to spread and infect more plants. There is considerable evidence that less crop damage occurs when various species are grown together.

Also, we often try to coax unwilling plants to grow in conditions that do not suit them. This is far removed from nature's 'law of the jungle', where each plant has to fight its neighbours to survive and only the fittest plants make it. Take a look sometime at the plants flourishing in some overgrown roadside verge. There is a tangled confusion of different species, but very few will show more than the most minor signs of leaf damage — quite a contrast with those cabbages in your garden, perhaps.

Nevertheless, anyone who has a garden wishes to exercise some degree of control over what grows in it and what eats it. Having said that, there are right ways and wrong ways to go about it.

Predictably enough, the insects come in for the first attacks. The use of insecticides is just too easy, but is about as subtle as trying to adjust a watch with a hammer and chisel. Suppose you spray insecticide on some plants under attack from aphids. You kill the aphids: great stuff, it works. You also kill the ladybirds and hoverflies which were feeding on the aphids. All the poison you spray eventually ends up in the soil, where it kills those insects which are supplying the soil with essential plant-growing elements by feeding on dead plant remains. Other types of beneficial soil organisms are also affected. Poisoned insects are eaten by birds, especially insects that did not receive a full, fatal dose. Those birds continue to eat poisoned insects in other gardens and many of the insecticides accumulate within the birds' bodies. Then clutches of eggs are laid which do not hatch, and eventually the birds are poisoned themselves.

Once in the soil, most insecticides stay there. They decompose very slowly and even when finally washed out by rain they only end up somewhere else: in a river or lake, or perhaps someone's drinking water. The manufacturers' claim that some of these insecticides are 'harmless when used as directed' is a rash one. Insecticides *are* harmful. Regular use can result in the accumulation of considerable concentrations in the soil, causing long-term if not permanent changes in it. The condition of the soil is so important, and its state of living balance so delicately poised, that it is foolish to treat it so crudely. Worse than this, high levels of insecticides have been analysed in food crops grown in such soils. Who is to say that they are harmless to us? Once

again, we try to over-simplify and make our lists of what is harmful and what is not.

Derris and pyrethrum are natural plant extracts which poison insects but do not persist for long in the soil, or harm birds; also, they are *relatively* harmless to us. They should be the first choice when things get desperate. It is necessary to look at the small print when buying, because they might be mixed with more undesirable substances.

There are various other alternatives to the use of persistent insecticides. A good remedy for aphids is to spray with water in which plenty of nettles have been soaked for at least five days. Caterpillars can be kept under control on cabbages by constantly checking the undersides of leaves for the eggs and crushing any that are found. Otherwise derris and pyrethrum can be used. Slug pellets are a hazard to

Slug

other animals which may eat them. A small bowl of beer sunk into the soil makes a highly effective slug trap; what a way to go! If you are too mean to use beer, water containing a mixture of sugar and bakers' yeast seems to work as well. If wood-ash, eggshells or chalk are sprinkled thickly round the plants in question, they will establish a slug-proof barrier.

Spiders

Insects and spiders have been enemies ever since the first animals left the swamps and began life on dry land. Much has been made of the first emergence of our repulsive, newt-like ancestor from the ancient lakes and creeks, but that came much later. In fact those first amphibians probably came out of the water to chase insects. It is likely that the ancestors of the spiders were there even before the insects.

Nobody knows how insects first developed wings, but one theory suggests that it was a result of being preyed on by spiders. Whether or not this is true, the spiders were quick enough to respond with the invention of intricate aerial webs.

Spiders have hard outside skeletons like insects, but have eight legs and a body divided into only two parts: there is no division between head and thorax. The rather similar harvestmen have a body in only one unit, with no waist. These are also insect eaters, rather slow-moving, with very long thin legs. The abundance of garden insects has been mentioned and spiders are also extremely numerous here. Over 600 British species of spider have been described and many more undoubtedly remain to be discovered, as likely as not in somebody's garden.

The garden spider (*Araneus diadematus*) is especially familiar and its circular orb-webs are to be seen in gardens everywhere. It waits hidden by a leaf or crevice from the view of hungry birds, one leg delicately holding a single strand of silk running out from the centre of the web. It looks like an angler fishing with a handline, waiting for a 'bite'. On

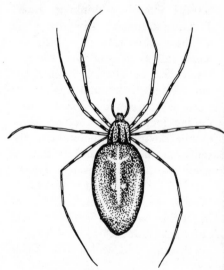

Garden spider (*Araneus diadematus*)

50

feeling a vibration, the spider rushes out, pounces on the trapped insect and bites it with its poisonous fangs. The insect may then be rolled up in silk and left for a later meal. The spider injects digestive juices then sucks out the liquefied insides. Webs are often made inside the windows of a garden shed where flies abound, and this is an ideal place to watch the whole drama.

Also in sheds are the spiders that make tangled cobwebs in corners, the various species of house spider (*Tegenaria spp*). This is the big spider that so often regards us balefully from the bottom of the bath. (On the basis of experimental work and discussions in the highest academic circles, the consensus of opinion is that most of them do *not* in fact climb up through the plughole, but fall into the bath from the edge or off the bathroom ceiling.)

Not all spiders build webs. Wolf spiders may be seen in dry, sunny parts of the garden. They run and pounce on insects before they have time to take flight and may sometimes be seen lying in ambush in flower heads that are attracting numbers of insect visitors. A female wolf spider may sometimes be seen carrying a large, white, silky ball under her abdomen. This is an egg cluster wrapped in a cocoon. The tiny young spiders will ride around on her back for the first few days after hatching. Spider eggs are normally protected by cocoons but left in secluded crevices.

Silk is put to so many uses by spiders. The tiny young of many species use it for flight, to enable them to disperse over a wide area. When conditions are just right, minute spiders everywhere climb upwards as high as they can before paying out a length of silk into the breeze. Then they let go and sail away like vast numbers of hot-air balloonists towards countless unknown destinies.

Amphibians and reptiles

When cleaning out a very small garden pond in the suburbs of Liverpool, I once found four large frogs. The pond measured 5 × 3ft, the garden was a small one, the entire district was completely built up and I knew of no other pond anywhere near. There was no possibility of anybody having put the frogs there. Those frogs can only have travelled from someone else's garden pond, presumably where they were born. Thanks to our gardens, the suburbs are often much wilder than we think.

The British amphibians are the frogs, toads and newts. All share the common feature of being restricted to the vicinity of a suitable breeding pond. Their eggs are laid in water, and their young pass through a tadpole stage. In addition to this, their delicate skins must always be kept fairly moist.

The common frog (*Rana temporaria*) is the species most likely to be seen. It is nowhere near as common as it was fifty years ago, and garden ponds are an increasingly important habitat for it. This is partly due to the 'development' of marshy areas, the widespread use of frogs for dissection

in schools several decades ago, and the use of agricultural insecticides: frogs eat insects.

Newts travel further from their watery breeding places. They are secretive, nocturnal animals which are seldom seen outside the spring breeding season, when they congregate to spawn in ponds. The smooth newt (*Triturus vulgaris*) is the species most commonly seen.

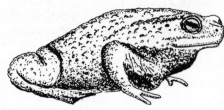

Common toad (*Bufo bufo*)

Toads are also much more independent of water then frogs, but they hide away by day in cool, damp places. At night they emerge and go off in search of insects. In the spring they migrate considerable distances to the breeding area. Many people have reported having the same resident toad for years, so they must often return to their territory. The common toad is *Bufo bufo*. But in that same small south Liverpool garden we were once visited by a scarce natterjack toad. This species has a distinctive yellow line down its back and one of its last strongholds in Britain is an area of sand dunes some twenty miles north of Liverpool. I have always wondered if it crossed the city centre on its own, or if somebody carried it.

Reptiles are distinguished from amphibians by their dry, scaly skins and by the fact that they do not lay their eggs in water. In contrast, reptiles have a positive liking for dry, warm places. They are cold-blooded animals and enjoy basking in the sunshine. The slow worm (*Anguis fragilis*) is particularly familiar. It may be found in most sunny, well-drained areas with plenty of undergrowth for it to hide in. It is probably commoner in rural gardens than suburban ones, and is a great help there because its principal food is slugs. Although it resembles a snake, it is actually a lizard with no legs. Adders and grass snakes have dark markings, but slow worms are an even brownish colour. They do not lay eggs, and their young are born alive.

Viviparous lizards (*Lacerta vivipara*) may also be seen in warm weather on drystone walls or stony banks with plenty of crevices. They also bear live young.

Adders and grass snakes are all too easily confused. The harmless grass snake (*Natrix natrix*) lives in marshy areas and feeds almost exclusively on frogs. The adder (*Vipera berus*) is Britain's only poisonous snake, but its bite, although painful, is very seldom fatal. A common British inshore sea fish (the weever) is much more venomous. Both snakes have rather variable markings and it is unreliable to rely on the often mentioned dark zig-zag on the back of the adder. A more constant feature is the yellowish patch round the throat of the grass snake, which an adder never has. Neither snake should be mistaken for the slow worm, which is evenly coloured. None of these animals should be persecuted.

Mammals

There is no prize for guessing why mammals are the most appealing type of wildlife: we are mammals ourselves. But outside the tropics wild mammals are pretty elusive creatures, and there are far fewer species of them around than birds, especially in built-up areas; so birdwatchers greatly outnumber mammal-watchers. Birds are so easy to observe because their ability to fly gives them the confidence to move about in the open during the daytime. In contrast, most British mammals are timid and nocturnal. For this very reason, though, there are usually far more species of wild mammals in a garden or park than people suspect.

The brown rat (*Rattus norvegicus*) can attain a body length of 11 inches, about the length of a cat, and has a tail almost as long again. There are two British rats, but this is the commoner. It has been associated with man since prehistoric times, though not by human choice. There are now said to be two rats for every human being on earth, and quite apart from the food they steal and spoil, they spread a number of unpleasant diseases. These include bubonic plague, the 'black death' that killed half the population of Europe in the Middle Ages and is transmitted by the rat flea. Brown rats are most closely associated with us in the winter. In spring and summer they spread out into the countryside. Again, they are much commoner than we realise and it can be an education to walk quietly through deserted city streets at sunrise in the summer, or to watch picnic areas and litter bins in a park at that time.

Brown rat (*Rattus norvegicus*)

The house mouse (*Mus musculus*) is another mammal associated closely with man. It is also a pest, spoiling food and spreading disease. They are greyish in colour, but many individuals live in the countryside and tend to be browner. There, they are likely to be confused with fieldmice (*Sylvaemus flavicollis*), which have tails distinctly darker above than below. Wood mice (*Sylvaemus sylvaticus*) also have two-coloured tails, but have large ears, and longer legs for climbing. Be kind to the last two species if they venture indoors: they are not the same sort of nuisance as the house mouse.

Voles are rather appealing little mammals, with their short, rounded faces. They are vegetarians, brownish in colour and very common, especially bank voles (*Clethryonomys glareolus*) and short-tailed voles (*Microtus agrestis*). These can be distinguished by the length of the tail, which is nearly as long as the body in the bank vole, and very short in the other species. Water voles (*Arvicola amphibius*) are larger; they inhabit water margins and are great swimmers. They are scarce in Scotland, where the smaller ground vole (*Arvicola terrestris*) is more common instead.

The shrews are another group of mouse-like animals, this time with extremely pointed faces. They are carnivorous and will tackle a wide range of small animals: for their size, they are the fiercest mammals in the world, making tigers look like tabby-cats. It is fortunate that they are so small. The water shrew (*Neomys fodiens*) is the biggest, with a body length of 3 or 4 inches. It occupies similar habitats to the water vole. The common shrew (*Sorex araneus*) is 2 to 3 inches long, excluding its tail. This animal is the usual cause of the squeaks and rustlings often heard in overgrown patches of ground. The pygmy shrew (*Sorex minutus*) is minute, about 2 inches long. All these mammals are equally active by day and night.

Moles (*Talpa europaea*) are generally classed as vermin, on account of the untidiness of the heaps of earth they throw up on our nice neat lawns. In fact they are much more of an ally, because they feed on a large variety of grubs and insects, many of which are damaging to plant roots. Large numbers of earthworms are also eaten, but there are plenty of these to spare in any garden. Molehills on the lawn can simply be stamped flat again, but if you are determined to be rid of them, pieces of calcium carbide pushed into the burrow will form an evil-smelling gas that will drive them away. Moles can be kept away from beds of young seedlings by pushing mothballs into the ground at intervals of 6 inches or so, to form another kind of smell barrier. Many mothballs contain persistent insecticides: only those containing camphor or naphthalene alone should be used.

Hedgehogs (*Erinaceus europaeus*)

Pygmy shrew (*Sorex minutus*)

55

need no description. They are relatively common in many suburban areas and often become garden residents. They assist by eating large numbers of slugs and insects. A saucer of milk put out at night is likely to be gratefully accepted and a hedgehog will usually turn it upside down afterwards in the hope of finding something else underneath. A cat will seldom do this, so we can tell who has had the milk.

Badgers (*Meles meles*) are big, hefty animals, over 2 feet long excluding the tail. If there is a badger sett nearby, they are very likely to honour you by visiting your garden at night. The sett is usually on sloping ground in the edge of a wood. Badgers eat worms and beetles and make small exploratory excavations wherever they go. They also make holes for their dung. A badger in a small, neat garden may seem to you worse than a bull in a china shop; you have to decide on your priorities and strengthen your fences if you dislike such visitors.

We now have two British squirrels, the red (*Sciurus vulgaris*) and the grey (*Neosciurus carolinensis*). The grey squirrel was introduced into Britain from America at the start of this century. Apparently, certain gentlefolk fancied having something else to shoot at. They are now rapidly displacing our native red squirrels from most parts of Britain, and are generally far more common. Although disliked by timber growers because they strip bark from trees, they do little harm in suburban areas and are frequent visitors to gardens and parks. For many people, their worst crime is to rob bird tables and the occasional bird's nest.

The red fox (*Vulpes vulpes*) has adapted well to the expansion of civilised man. He has lived an outlaw existence on the fringes of our territory, plundering our refuse and our livestock. Foxes are now on the increase in cities and suburbs, being secretive and cunning enough to escape detection right under our noses. Railway embankments are a particular blessing to them. Contrary to popular belief, they do not live on an exclusive diet of farmers' chickens. Mice, voles, small birds and even beetles make up a large part of their diet, together with the contents of dustbins.

The garden at night

After dark, the garden is a different world. With hungry birds asleep, all sorts of tiny creatures emerge from hiding and go about their business. Garden spiders are out, each making a new web for the next day's insect-catching. Even the air sometimes smells different because certain flowers, such as honeysuckle, release more scent at dusk. These plants are relying on moths to transfer their pollen, and moths seem to be everywhere on a calm summer's night. Nobody really seems to know why they congregate around street lights and lighted windows. Some species are known to navigate by the position of the moon and this fact may be relevant. Flying at a certain angle to the moon would take a moth in a straight line from A to B. But flying at the same constant angle to a street light would cause it to spiral inwards, ever closer to it.

A simple moth trap can be set up on a window ledge using a biscuit tin with a light bulb inside and sliding glass cover. Cardboard egg-boxes inside provide shelter from the heat of the light bulb and persuade the moths to sit still. The tremendous variety of moths captured is amazing, wherever the trap is set up. Before releasing them they can be admired and identified if a suitable book is available. An interesting project is to take samples all year round and draw graphs of variations in total catches and the number of different species in them.

It is not necessary to watch the crowd of moths round a street light for long before noticing the first bat swoop through it. Bats and moths, just like the insects and the spiders, have been running an 'arms race' for millions of years. Bats evolved 'sonar', the ability to navigate and to locate their prey by interpreting the returning echoes of their own squeaks. Some moths responded by developing a 'jamming' system, confusing the bats by sending back similar squeaks of their own. In general moths have learned to respond to the approach of a bat by folding their wings and dropping like a stone out of harm's way. They do this on hearing the bat's squeaks. These squeaks are too high-pitched for most people to hear. In fact they are similar to the sounds emitted by those hand-held devices used to control television sets at a distance. Next time a moth flies in through an open window at night, point the device at it and fire away. Instant aerobatics at your command: better than television.

Outside, a torch beam reveals a lot of activity on the garden path. Beetles, woodlice, slugs and snails are out at work in such numbers that it is hard to imagine where they all hide in the daytime.

Woodlice are not insects, a fact at once betrayed by their many legs. They are one of the few land-dwelling crustaceans, the large group including crabs and shrimps. A number of species are commonly seen in gardens, often hiding under pieces of rotting wood to avoid drying out, which is fatal to them. They are extremely important members of the garden economy, feeding on dead plant matter and returning essential elements to the soil.

Slugs are snails which have no shells. Their slime is their protection and birds seldom attack them. Various true snails are common, but the only big one usually seen is the garden snail (*Helix pomatia*), the favourite food of thrushes. These snails often return to the same hideaway at daybreak, sometimes sharing it with many others.

The surprising variety of all these nocturnal wanderers can be demonstrated if you set pitfall traps consisting of buried jam jars. Prop up a piece of wood or slate to keep rain out if you want your catch alive and undrowned. A single wolf spider will cause such carnage that it is no less humane to cover the bottom of the jar with 70 per cent industrial alcohol (from the chemist) to kill and preserve all specimens caught.

On the lawn, the torch beam catches another movement. An earthworm retreats sharply into its burrow and disappears. Further searching soon reveals other worms stretched out on the grass, each with its tail in its burrow, ready to pull itself out of sight in a flash at a heavy footfall or if the torch illuminates it too brightly. Some of these worms are searching for fallen leaves, which they pull, tip first, into the upper part of their burrows and leave to await a future mealtime. Others are looking for a mate. Each worm is both male and female and the production of a cocoon of fertilised eggs is a complicated joint effort.

Worms are the most universal angling bait for all freshwater fish and can be collected without digging on a suitable summer night. The torch beam should be dimmed by stretching a handkerchief across it, to avoid alarming the worms; tread softly and grab them quickly where their bodies are next to their burrows. Do not tug a worm or it will break, because it holds on to the burrow tightly with its many short bristles. Keep up a steady pressure and the worm will let go in a few seconds.

Owls are heard more than they are seen, especially the tawny owl (*Strix aluco*) in suburban areas. No tawny owl goes 'Too-whit, too-whoo' as the common version gives it. At any one time, they either go 'Too-whit' *or* 'Too-whoo'. The cries are so very different that they sound like two different species. The idea is to demonstrate their territory to other owls and they will eagerly reply if you can imitate the call well enough. It can be considerably more entertaining if you have the chance to send out replies to other human owl-impersonators. Owls eat moths, beetles and small mammals.

Hedgehogs, badgers and even foxes can sometimes be attracted to food put out regularly within view of the window of a darkened room. Your local cats will probably have a ball, but you might feel it is worth it.

2
POND AND STREAM

Children have always been fascinated by the teeming underwater life of ponds, ditches and streams. Any summer's day you can watch the jamjar brigade poking with nets in the murky water of the local park. A survey at a symposium at Oxford once indicated that a large percentage of eminent zoologists could trace the origin of their careers to an early interest in pond life.

Junior pondhunting still thrives on a vast, international scale; is it the stirring of a primitive hunting instinct or some mysterious memory of our aquatic ancestors?

One of the attractions is that the world of freshwater animals is so accessible. The many forms of pond and stream life are amazingly widespread, so that in the country you need look no further than the nearest weed-choked pool or water-filled ditch. Even in towns many parks have boating lakes or some sort of ornamental pool or watercourse that is full of underwater wildlife. Very few homes are far away from ideal freshwater habitats, although the 'typical' countryside pond that we all imagine is fast disappearing. We

visualise a rustic pond in the corner of a field, shaded by trees and with part of the margin conveniently freed from choking vegetation by the trampling of drinking cattle: farmers get government grants for filling in such ponds and many others have vanished beneath new housing estates.

In some unfortunate areas there may be little sign of life in water contaminated by the chemical waste of factories, or in streams suffocated by decaying sewage or agricultural waste like silage. The very justifiable fuss being made about pollution must not blind us to the fact that many freshwater habitats are alive and well in most areas. We are often too ready to write them off as polluted. For example, the word 'stagnant' has unpleasant overtones, yet there is no harm or health risk in stagnant water in this country, unless you drink it. Whatever your feelings about the water beneath an unbroken scum of duckweed, it is a natural, healthy, balanced environment and harmful substances will only be present if they have been introduced by man. Similarly, very few streams contain sewage. If you find one that does, inform the local Water Authority.

This chapter has been entitled *Pond and Stream* because these are so much more numerous and accessible than lakes and rivers. Even so, much of what is said here is also applicable to the shallow margins of lakes and rivers, provided that certain differences are borne in mind. Anything more than a stream or a small pond is likely to contain much larger fish than the familiar minnows and sticklebacks. Many lakes are so deep that insufficient light reaches the bottom to support plants, so their underwater scenery consists of dim plains of flat mud. Countless species live exclusively in this mysterious domain and many new ones undoubtedly await discovery, (possibly including the Loch Ness Monster).

Another difference with these larger bodies of water will be noticed if you poke about in the rocky margin of a lake. The creatures you find there bear more resemblance to the inhabitants of a fast stream than to those of a pond, many of them clinging tightly to the stones. This is because large waves frequently cause violent water movements at the edge of a lake.

The smaller bodies of fresh water, the ponds, streams and ditches of our land, can be explored by anybody almost anywhere. There is no need to travel far, no costly equipment is necessary, and all sorts of fascinating organisms are easy to catch and study. It is a world about which a tremendous amount remains to be discovered, though several research establishments are devoted entirely to it.

How to collect pond and stream animals

A large selection of pond and stream animals can be found simply by grubbing around with your bare hands at the water's edge, but collecting is far more productive with suitable equipment. A useful and professional-looking collecting kit can easily be put together.

Top of the list comes some sort of shallow, watertight container in which to sort specimens from mud and weed. It must provide a pale-coloured background to help you spot small creatures in a centimetre or so of muddy water. The bigger the better, but it has to be small enough to carry about. The shallow type of white plastic ice-cream box is just about big enough; a white plastic tray as supplied for photographic darkrooms is even better.

A teaspoon and a cheap little paintbrush are useful for handling specimens. Try to get hold of a couple of pipettes from a chemist's shop — short glass tubes with a small rubber teat at one end and a narrow 'nozzle' at the other. Two pipettes are best, one with a fine nozzle for very small animals and the other without. A nozzle can be reversed and stuck inside the teat, or it may be carefully snapped off and the sharp glass rounded off by heating in a gas flame.

A magnifying glass will often be useful. It need not be particularly powerful: ×5 is strong enough. Strong lenses need to be held very close to the specimen, which can be awkward if it is under water. A lens which folds away into a protective cover is a good idea.

A glass jam jar makes a convenient waterside aquarium in which to study individual creatures, with or without a magnifying glass. A couple of screw-topped jam jars are also useful for carrying specimens.

The best way to take home a wide variety of smaller specimens is to obtain a dozen or so proper specimen tubes. These are like small bottles of glass or clear plastic which do not become narrower at the top and have tight-fitting stoppers or screw-on caps. If you can't find a dealer in laboratory equipment, try a chemist or visit a hypochondriac relative, because many plastic pill-containers are suitable.

A handful of smallish polythene bags with some wire fasteners will

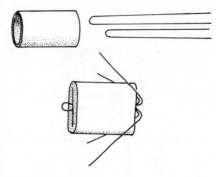

Making a weed drag

enable plants to be taken home for closer examination or for an aquarium. An inexpensive cloth bag with a shoulder strap is necessary to carry this lot.

A weed drag is another indispensible piece of equipment (see diagram). Bend in half two 8 inch lengths cut from a wire coathanger and push them into a 2 inch length of lead or copper pipe. Bash the pipe completely flat with a heavy hammer and bend the four prongs into position. If you leave a loop of wire projecting from the other end of the flattened tube, a length of strong cord can be tied to it, then wound on to a square piece of wood. Something nearly identical costs several pounds from a supplier of biological equipment.

The drag is used to capture the many organisms that inhabit weedbeds. First, half-fill the plastic ice-cream box with pond water, then unwind a suitable length of cord and heap it neatly on the ground. Holding one end of the cord, throw the weed drag into the weedbed you wish to sample. If all goes well you should be able to haul in a fair-sized lump of weed. Pull it in as fast as possible, before too many of the more active animals have a chance to escape. Lift out the mass of weed and dump as much of it as you can into the box of water. Unless you particularly want to examine the various inhabitants of mud, try to keep the plant roots out because they cloud the water. Shake the weed vigorously for a while, then lay it aside. With any luck your catch will contain a surprisingly wide variety of animals and you can sit down to sort them out. Some likely finds are described on pages 70–4.

This is the simplest way to catch small freshwater creatures in ponds, ditches and slow streams. By moving around it is interesting to compare the animals inhabiting different species of weedbed living at different depths. This method is only likely to fail to produce impressive results in winter, when many water plants die back and the populations of small animals are greatly reduced.

Various species of minute animals spend most of their time swimming and drifting mid-water, often well

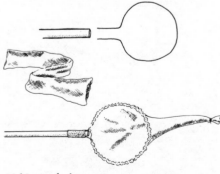

Making a plankton net

away from weedbeds. They are collectively known as 'plankton', a term also applied to the minute drifting creatures of the open sea. A very effective plankton net can be made from the leg of a pair of nylon tights (see diagram). Bend a loop about 5 inches across from some more coathanger wire or something similar. Bind it securely to a 4 foot bamboo cane, using many tight turns of plastic insulation tape. Cut an 18 inch length from one leg of the tights and stitch it to the wire frame. Close the other end of the net, tying it off with thread. Do not make the net any shorter than specified or water will not flow fast enough through the mesh, producing an underwater 'bow wave'.

To sample an area of water, the plankton net is moved continuously to and fro for a while, in a figure-of-eight pattern. The knack is quickly acquired with practice. The catch is removed by turning the net inside out and immersing the end in a couple of inches of water in a jam jar or the sorting tray. The abundance of freshwater plankton varies a lot from place to place, even in the same pond, but the net will sometimes come out bulging. The several species of small crustaceans called 'water fleas' (see pages 70–4) usually make up the bulk of the catch, together with a selection of small insect larvae and a few beetles.

This net can also be used to catch larger individual animals, including insects on the surface film, and to dredge samples from the surface of the bottom mud.

Here is a simple checklist of pond-hunters' equipment, capable of sampling most forms of freshwater life.

Sorting tray (ice-cream box or tub); teaspoon; paintbrush; narrow-mouthed and wide-mouthed pipette; magnifying lens; two screw-topped jam jars; specimen tubes or plastic pill-boxes; polythene bags; bag; weed drag; plankton net.

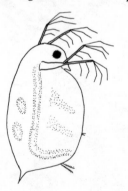
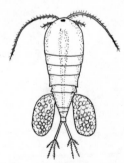

Common plankton animals: *Daphnia* (*left*), *Cyclops* and phantom midge larva (*below*)

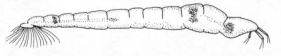

66

Water plants

There are two main categories of water plants. The simplest ones are the microscopic algae that sometimes form slimy green masses, or give a green tinge to mud or even to the water itself. The algae are more fully described in a later section. Most of the remaining water plants belong to the same group as the land plants, with stems, roots, leaves and flowers. In the summer, ponds, streams and ditches usually support a rampant confusion of plant life along their margins and beneath the water's surface. Quite apart from its own interest, the luxuriant growth should be investigated because of the tremendous amount of small animal life that shelters in it.

Even some distance back from the water's edge the soil is permanently moist. Low, green clumps of rushes are everywhere, together with various colourful flowers. The elegant yellow flag iris is one of the brightest of these.

The plants right at the water's edge are content to grow 'with their feet in the water'. Most are tall and well rooted in the mud. The common reed is very widespread, pencil-thin yet taller than a man and with its feathery flowers swaying gracefully in the breeze. The bulrush (*Schoenoplectus lacustris*) is also common here but presents us with a naming problem. The familiar, brown-clubbed plant

Common reed (*Phragmites communis*) (*left*) and reedmace (*Typha latifolia*)

67

also seen in this habitat, and always shown in old pictures of the infant Moses, is *not* the bulrush, insist the botanists: it is the reedmace (*Typha latifolia*).

Other plants grow underwater in the shallows, yet tend to form masses of floating leaves and flowers. The water lilies are the largest, with almost circular leaves and big beautiful waxy flowers. There are two common species, the white water lily (*Nymphaea alba*) and the yellow (*Nuphar lutea*).

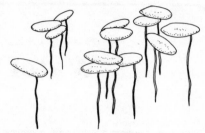

Duckweed (*above*)

Tangled masses of starwort (*Callitriche verna*) are often topped with floating leaves in shallow water. It is a very common plant with a long, slender stem and leaves in opposite pairs, forming star-shaped rosettes at the surface. The broad-leaved pondweed (*Potamogeton natans*) has larger, oval, floating leaves. In some places the surface may be covered with the floating leaves and white flowers of various species of water crowfoot. These plants, along with many other water plants, produce two distinct shapes of leaf. There is a rounded floating type and a finely divided submerged version which gives the plant its name.

Water plants obtain a large proportion of the materials they need directly from the water. Their roots are not as important as those of land plants. Some species are therefore able to live afloat on the water surface with no firm anchorage. The little duckweed plants are familiar examples, often forming an unbroken green film over the surface. A root hangs down from

Water milfoil (*Myriophyllum* spp) (*top*) and hornwort (*Ceratophyllum* spp)

68

each tiny plant, absorbing essential dissolved chemicals from the water. There are also larger floating plants such as the frogbit (*Hydrocharis morsusranae*), with a rosette of circular leaves, and water soldier (*Stratiotes aloides*), with long, spiky leaves.

The hornworts are fully submerged plants which lack roots and have straight, slender stems and whorls of narrow leaves. They often float freely in a vertical position.

There are many species of fully submerged plants which form dense beds deeply rooted in the bottom mud. The water milfoils are attractive, with reddish stems and feathery leaves. They make good aquarium plants. So does the Canadian pondweed (*Elodea canadensis*). This very common plant looks rather like the starwort, but is darker green and more brittle. Although common now, this plant was unknown in Britain at the beginning of the previous century.

Where submerged water plants are absent from unpolluted water, it is usually because of lack of light. They will not receive enough light if the water is too deep, or if mud is stirred up constantly, perhaps by cattle or boats. In other places a surface layer of duckweed may critically reduce light penetration.

The ability of a body of water to support plant growth is closely related to the amount of animal life it can feed. It has been mentioned that water plants are an important form of shelter

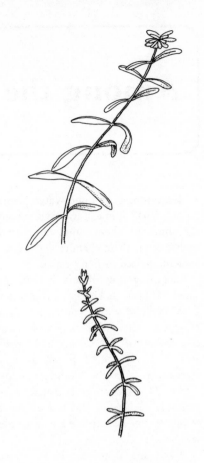

Starwort (*Callitriche* spp) (*top*) and Canadian pondweed (*Elodea canadensis*)

for small animals. More than this, those humble microscopic plants — the algae — are the basic source of food for the entire freshwater community. These algae are the freshwater equivalent of the grass on the African plains which effectively supports everything from antelope to lions and vultures.

Among the water plants

A dense jungle of underwater plants attracts small animals: it provides food for some of them, and most find shelter from their enemies and a convenient surface to hang on to.

Imagining now that a handful of weed has been shaken in a little water in a shallow white container, then removed, there follows a general description of the commonest small animals likely to be found as you search about in the slightly muddy water. This technique is usually surprisingly successful, but not *all* these creatures can be expected in a single sample.

Water snails are usually abundant on water plants. There are a great many different species and many of them grow no larger than a fraction of a centimetre. The wandering snail (*Lymnaea peregra*) is the commonest, with a broad-mouthed shell rather less than 2 cm long. The various species of ramshorn snails will be familiar to aquarium owners. These have shells that coil in a flat spiral. The biggest snail is the great pond snail (*Lymnaea stagnalis*) which grows to over 5 cm in length. Some snails will eat water plants, but their main food consists of the coating of microscopic green algae. The rasping mouth of a snail can be seen in action against the glass of a jam jar or aquarium. Snail eggs often appear on the glass of an aquarium in the form of masses of clear jelly full of tiny specks of life.

The active little water beetles are immediately noticeable. Most aquatic insects are just young larval forms that develop into flying adults, but water beetles spend much of their time under water, even though they are capable of flying. There is a huge number of different species and some are carnivorous, others vegetarians. The biggest is the great diving beetle (*Dytiscus marginalis*) which is over 3 cm long. Many others are very small.

Water beetles breathe air from the surface and a silvery bubble of air is often visible, trapped against the abdomen, as the beetle struggles against the extra buoyancy of this reserve supply.

The young larvae of water beetles are variable in shape, but are basically elongated, segmented and with shortish legs. These larvae normally crawl out of the water before emerging from their skins as adult water beetles. (This should be borne in mind if this transformation is to be followed in an aquarium.)

The damselflies are one of the many insect groups which spend their early life underwater, feeding and growing before changing into non-aquatic winged adults. Damselfly larvae are fairly common amongst water plants, where they live as carnivores preying on all sorts of smaller animals. They can be recognised by the three leaf-shaped gills at the rear of the long abdomen. Eventually, the fully grown larva crawls out of the water and sheds its dowdy skin to reveal an adult insect of glittering beauty. There are a number of species, but most are highly colourful with narrow, metallic-coloured bodies a couple of inches long. Some have transparent wings which become invisible in flight. Others have coloured wings and flutter like butterflies. In the summer it is common to see mating

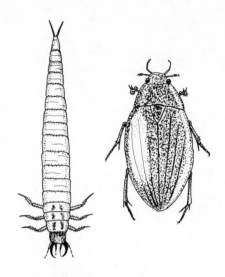

Water beetle: larva (*left*) and adult

pairs flying joined together.

Damselflies attack smaller insects resting on the waterside vegetation. They are close relatives of the much larger, fiercer dragonflies whose larvae live in the mud at the bottom of the

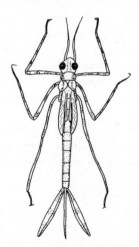

Damselfly: larva (*left*) and adult

71

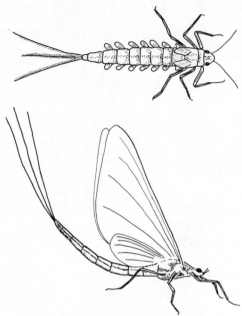

Mayfly: larva (*top*) and adult

pond, and are described later.

The largest species of mayfly have bodies up to 2 cm long and large wings and tails, but these are only locally common. There are numerous smaller species to be found almost everywhere. Both adults and larvae can be recognised by the characteristic group of three long tail appendages. (Mayfly larvae can be distinguished from damselfly larvae by the length and thinness of these tail appendages, and by the presence of gills along the sides of the abdomen.)

Although the mayfly larva may live and grow for a year or so, the story that the adults often lay their eggs and die within twenty-four hours of emerging from their larval skin is perfectly true. Their up-and-down mating flights can often be seen.

The larvae of the moth-like caddis fly live in all sorts of freshwater environments. There are many different species. Most are characterised by a tubular 'shell' made from stones, sandgrains, twigs or pieces of water plant. The larva drags this around and retreats into it when danger threatens.

The sluggish, but fearsome-looking water scorpion is about 3 cm long and as carnivorous as it looks. It resembles a dead leaf when it lies in ambush in shallow water. The long breathing tube at its rear end is used to supply air from the surface.

There seems to be widespread confusion between the water boatman and insects like the pond skater which live on the surface film. The various species of water boatmen live underwater. Propelled by their oar-like legs, they are more like 'rowing submarines'. They are extremely common and there are two main groups. The true water boatmen swim on their backs with a silvery film of air covering their belly. They are carnivorous, and the piercing mouthparts of the larger species are quite capable of pricking a finger. The other group, the lesser water boatmen, swim the right way up and feed on the surface of the mud, sucking up the organic matter.

Sometimes a tiny bright-red speck will be seen swimming around with a wandering, wavering motion. This is a water mite. Not all species are red, others are bright green or pale brown. Unlike the other creatures described, these are not insects. Close examination reveals four pairs of legs, indicat-

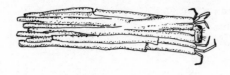

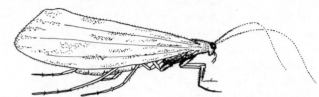

Caddis fly: larva in case (*top*) and adult

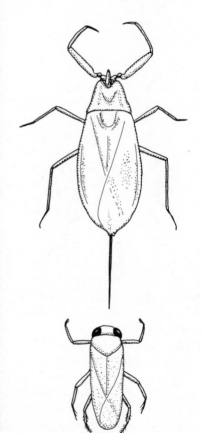

Water Scorpion (*Nepa cinerea*) (*top*) and lesser
water boatman (*Corixa* spp)

ing that they belong to the same
group as the spiders, the Arachnids.
They are carnivorous, devouring any
minute animals they encounter.

Water lice and freshwater shrimps
are not insects either but crustaceans
(see page 20). The water louse
resembles its more heavily built
relative, the woodlouse. The freshwater shrimp also has too many legs
to be an insect, and is flattened from
side to side, unlike the water louse
which is flattened from top to
bottom. It is not a true shrimp, being
more closely related to the sandhoppers which swarm in rotting seaweed on the seashore. Water lice and
freshwater shrimps are both common
in weedbeds. They are general
scavengers.

Flatworms have the appearance of
brown or grey oblong smudges, a
centimetre or so in length (see page
44). They glide smoothly and quite
rapidly along the bottom of the
sorting tray. The mouth is midway
along the undersurface and they are
mainly carnivorous. It is easy to
capture them by setting a bait, such as
a piece of meat tied to a string, leaving

73

it for a while, then pulling it out and washing off the flatworms.

The various species of leech look vaguely similar to flatworms until they start to move. They get about by means of suckers at the front and back end, with highly characteristic 'looping' movements. All are carnivorous, and many species suck the blood of larger animals. Only the medicinal leech can pierce human skin. This species is only found in a few areas and is easily recognised by its large size (over 10 cm). Some leeches may be seen swimming with vigorous up-and-down undulations of their bodies.

Water mites

Hydras are minute animals related to the jellyfish and anemones of the seashore. There are several species, but they are not likely to be found during routine collecting, because they are hard to see.

Hydras feed on small creatures such as water fleas and they are ideal specimens for the 'window-ledge zoo' and for observation with a microscope.

The best way to collect them is to place various samples of water plants in a number of jam jars of pond water and leave for a few days. Hydras may often then be seen on the sides of some of the jars. Their thin bodies are usually about 1 cm long when extended and very thin tentacles hang down from the end. The green hydra, is attracted to light, so partial shading of the jars can make them move.

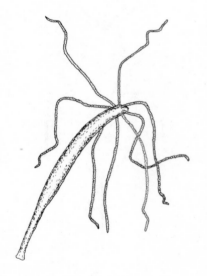

Hydra

Amongst the stones of fast streams

There is no hard and fast division between the creatures and plants of still-water habitats such as ponds and ditches, and those of the running water of rivers and streams. Many species are found in both. The previous section described the animals likely to be encountered while searching amongst the water plants of ponds. Nearly all these will also be found in the shelter of weedbeds in slow flowing streams. There is little difference as far as many animals are concerned, although certain species do show a marked preference for either still or flowing water.

Nevertheless there are considerable differences between the conditions in a pond and those in a fast flowing stream. As we look at the characteristics and inhabitants of a fast stream, we have to bear in mind that at various times we are likely to find every intermediate stage between the two extremes represented by fast flowing and static water.

First, a current washes away soil and mud, leaving a bed of stones or gravel. Water plants are only able to grow in areas sheltered from the main current, but dark green growths of water moss cover many of the larger stones. A strong current presents problems to animals as well. Only fish, such as trout, minnows, loach and bullheads have sufficient strength to swim against it. The smaller creatures have only two choices if they are not to be swept away helplessly. They can cling tightly to the stones, or shelter below them from the main force of current. Many do both. Many of the mayfly larvae found here are extremely flattened, of a shape allowing the current to press them tightly against the stones.

There are two compensating benefits for the inhabitants of fast streams. For one thing, there is no need to

Water moss (*Fontinalis* spp)

75

venture far in search of food. Decaying plant fragments, algae, microorganisms and small, dislodged creatures are swept constantly past. A number of specialised fast-water animals build nets and traps to make use of this free food supply.

The other advantage is the large amount of dissolved oxygen in the water. This gas, essential to animals, can often become scarce in stagnant water. But here the splashing and turbulence constantly replenish the supply. Many fast-water species are unable to live for long in jam jars or aquaria without strong aeration.

We can easily find out what animals live here by looking beneath stones, carefully replacing them afterwards. As a stone is lifted, many specimens remain clinging tightly to its lower surface. Others may be swept away downstream into a suitably positioned hand net.

When a stone is lifted from the stream bed the attention is often caught by the wriggling movements of small mayfly larvae in the film of water beneath it. There are many species and they are not likely to be the same as those found in still water, although they share the same characteristics: three long tails, and gill-fringed bodies. The fact that many remain on the stone when it is pulled out of the stream demonstrates how well they can cling to it to resist the current. The flattened shape of many fast-water mayfly larvae is ideal for their clinging existence.

Stonefly larvae are common in running water and resemble mayfly

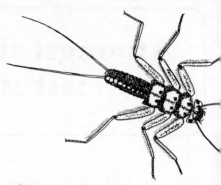

Stonefly larva

larvae at first glance. However, they only have two tails and lack the well developed gills of the mayflies. Their rudimentary gills restrict them to habitats with high oxygen levels: they are not found in ponds and are hard to keep in captivity. Certain species are found amongst the stones on the wave-washed shores of lakes, a habitat similar in many ways to fast streams. (There are many other similarities between the populations of certain lake margins and rocky streams.) As with mayflies, identifying the various species of stoneflies is a task for the specialists.

Freshwater shrimps will also often be noticed on the undersides of stones, skipping about on their sides in their familiar way. There are only a couple of species and the ones you find are probably of the same species, (*Gammarus pulex*) that is most common in still water.

Tiny, dark, elongated snails less than half a centimetre long are often common. This is Jenkins' spire shell, (*Potamopyrgus jenkinsi*) which represents something of a snail success

Freshwater algae under the microscope

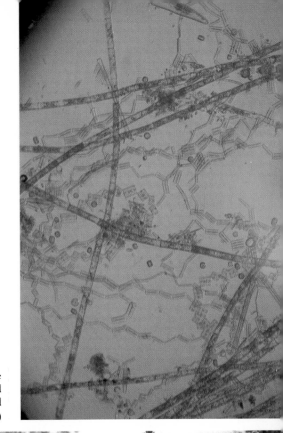

Fenland pond with a clump of purple loosestrife, and the leathery, heart-shaped leaves of the yellow water lily on the pond surface (*Leslie Jackman/Wildlife Picture Agency*)

(*Above*) Young spring growth at the edge of a freshwater marsh, showing ferns and flag spikes appearing (*Rodger Jackman/Wildlife Picture Agency*)

(*Opposite*) Fast flowing stream in a field, bordered by the yellow flag, wild relative of familiar garden irises (*John Beach/Wildlife Picture Agency*)

(*Below*) Water ditch showing reddish deposits from the oxidisation of iron salts (from surrounding soil) by bacteria. This indicates low oxygen levels, unsuitable for much animal life, but the process encourages the growth of algae (*David Cayless/Wildlife Picture Agency*)

Pond with floating leaves of white water lily, marginal growth of common reed and domesticated muscovy ducks

Pond skater, an insect which lives on the water surface, a fierce predator of smaller insects

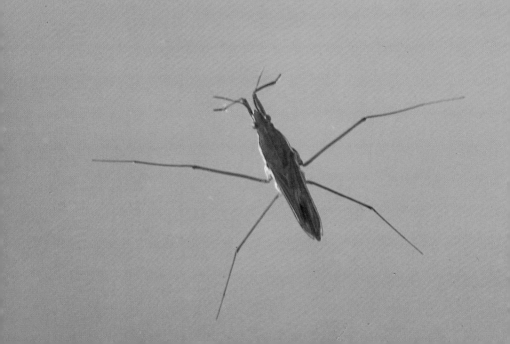

story. At the end of last century this snail was unknown in fresh water, and lived only in the brackish water of estuaries. For some unknown reason it has suddenly invaded rivers and streams and is now just about the commonest snail in running water. Various other snails will also be seen, mostly small ones. Among them are various species of ramshorn snails with their flattened, 'catherine wheel' shells.

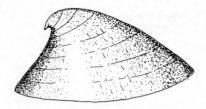

River limpet (*Ancylastrum fluviatile*)

Better adapted for clinging to stones in very fast currents is the river limpet (*Ancylastrum fluviatile*) with its small conical shell, well under a centimetre long. A related species is found in the margins of lakes.

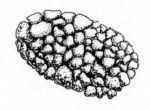

Case of a fast-water caddis larva fastened to a stone

Less likely to catch the eye when examining a stone are the soft, flattened bodies of flatworms and leeches, but several species of each are common. Although similar in outline, flatworms and leeches are different animals, and can be instantly distinguished as soon as they move. A leech will usually search from side to side with its pointed front end, while its broader rear remains firmly attached to the stone. Finally it will take hold with the front sucker and move off with its unmistakable 'looping' action. The various flatworm species all glide along smoothly rather like snails.

Little clusters, a centimetre or two long, formed by numbers of tiny pebbles, are often seen on stones from a stream bed. They are the homes of highly specialised caddis larvae which have given up any idea of carrying their homes around and fasten them-

selves down in a fixed position instead. They then rely on the current to bring them an adequate supply of food. As we saw, the various species of caddis larvae found in still-water weedbeds normally occupy tubular mobile homes made of pieces of water plants. Mobile caddis larvae are also found in quite fast streams, but their 'homes' are more often heavier affairs made of small pebbles. It is not just a question of the shortage of water plants: heavy structures are a definite advantage where there is any risk of being swept away downstream.

Comparing the inhabitants of ponds and streams like this can illustrate how all living creatures have adapted to the particular ways of life they lead.

The various species of blackfly have a larval stage which is particularly well adapted for life in fast water. Large numbers of the larvae, which

81

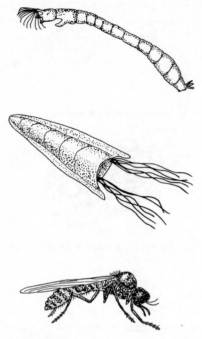

Blackfly (*Simulium* spp): larva (*top*), pupa and adult (*below*)

look rather like tiny caterpillars just over a centimetre long, may be seen clinging to stones, branches and water plants, often where the current is strongest. They sieve out their food from the water with comb-like bristles at the front end, while firmly anchored down by the rear end. If dislodged, they move with a looping action that heightens their resemblance to certain caterpillars.

When the larvae have become pupae, the waiting stage before the emergence of the winged adults, they look totally different, like dark little cones cemented firmly against any solid object. The wide end of each cone always faces into the current. When the adult fly emerges from the pupal skin, it has no time to waste before it escapes from the swirling torrent at the surface. It bursts free and bobs to the surface surrounded by a bubble of air. Popping out through the surface film, it flies away instantly.

This insect, again, is wonderfully adapted to its environment. The adult fly, however, has a fearful reputation as a biter. I had an unpleasant encounter with a particularly nasty species of blackfly once while clipping a hedge in the North of Scotland. Large numbers must have been resting in the hedge, because they emerged from the clippings on the ground and went up the legs of my jeans. Surprisingly I felt nothing during the attack, presumably because of the anaesthetic injected by the mouthparts of many bloodsuckers. A chemical which prevents clotting and keeps the blood flowing is also injected, and the first I knew about it was that I noticed that my socks were soaked with blood. Marks were still visible on my legs six months later, and I have had a healthy respect for blackflies ever since.

On the water surface

Water has certain peculiar properties which we, as large animals, seldom notice. Small pond creatures experience it as a very different substance. A bather can swim to the edge of a swimming pool and hoist himself out casually. Think about that next time you help a drowning fly out of a pool of water. If you just push the fly to the edge, it will often be unable to drag itself out. The water clings to it and seems to be dragging it back. The surface curves and is pulled up as the insect heaves — and insects, for their size, are the strongest creatures in the world. It is as if the water has a surface skin which will not break and will not release the waterlogged creature.

This is the phenomenon of 'surface tension', a mere curiosity to us, but a ruling factor in the lives of many small water creatures. It has its uses as well as its dangers for some of them. Certain insects can walk on the surface film without breaking through it and getting wet. Just try doing *that* at the swimming baths. The secret, apart from being of small size, is to have a waxy covering on the body to which water will not stick, and to have pads

of similarly waxy bristles on the feet to avoid breaking through the surface. Insect species equipped to 'walk on the water' in this way can be seen everywhere in the summer, in ditches, the margins of ponds and the sheltered areas of slow flowing water at the edges of streams.

However, most insects do not have this ability to anything like the same degree. For them, the surface of the water can be a death-trap because once they break through that strange 'skin' it holds them and drags them down. Small insects are so abundant at the waterside that the surface is often covered with struggling or dead individuals who have become trapped. These unfortunate insects are the main food of the water-walkers. Their drowning struggles send out widening circles of tiny ripples. The carnivores of the surface film are highly sensitive to these and know instantly where any surface disturbance is coming from. In this way they locate their prey.

The pond skaters are perhaps the commonest creatures of this type. There are a number of species and their long legs make them look quite

83

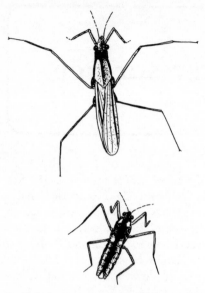

big. All insects, of course, have six legs yet at first glance the pond skaters seem only to have four. A closer look shows that the front pair of legs are short and powerful, held at the ready in front for grabbing hold of struggling prey.

The water crickets, dark brown with orange markings, are commonest on running water.

The water measurer is just over a centimetre long and extremely thin. Its name comes from the slow, deliberate way it paces across the surface. It is less commonly seen than the skaters and water crickets.

The three groups mentioned above are all 'bugs'. The characteristic features of this group are the piercing, tubular mouthparts designed to suck out the soft insides of their prey. The whirligig beetles belong to an entirely different order of insects, with their typical beetle-type hard wing-cases.

Pond skater (*Gerris* spp) (*top*) and water cricket (*Velia* spp); (*below*) water measurer (*Hydrometra stagnorum*)

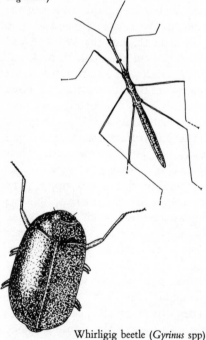

Whirligig beetles are incredibly active. They first resemble swarms of small, shiny ball-bearings skimming over the surface in mazy zig-zags. When you stoop for a closer look they dive beneath the surface and vanish. They feed on dead and drowning insects, but their 'ripple-sense' has an added refinement. Their swimming activity sends out minute, buzzing ripples, and they can detect and decode the patterns made when these ripples are reflected back from objects on the surface. It is a kind of 'ripple radar', which explains how they can locate dead as well as struggling insects. It also explains how these astonishing insects avoid bumping

Whirligig beetle (*Gyrinus* spp)

into one another. In addition to whizzing about on the surface and swimming underwater, whirligig beetles can also crawl about on dry land and occasionally fly.

Mosquitoes, or gnats, lay their eggs on the water and their larvae remain attached to the underside of the surface film until they are ready to shed their skin and fly off as adults. Although mosquito larvae are often seen in ponds, it is easy to observe them by simply leaving a container of water out in your garden during the summer. Tiny, boat-shaped rafts of dark-coloured eggs will almost always appear at the edge of the water. These soon hatch into elongated larvae which hang, head down, from the surface. They breathe through their tails but will quickly let go and wriggle down through the water when you approach too closely.

After a few weeks their shape changes. They appear to have a big 'head' with a small tail curled beneath. They continue to hang beneath the surface, diving down with rapid spinning movements when disturbed. These are the pupae and they do not feed. They are gradually changing inside in preparation for the moment when the adult mosquito will burst out and fly away.

To put two or three larvae in a jam jar of water from the place you captured them must be the easiest way to watch the development of a young insect. They will feed on microscopic plants and animals in the water.

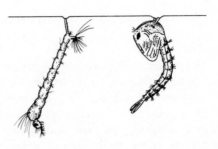

Mosquito: adult (*top*), larva (*left*) and pupa

Cover the jar with muslin so that you can see the adults when they emerge.

Certain mosquitoes commonly transmit malaria to humans in warmer climates, and certain areas of Britain also suffered from this in the past. Nowadays it is extremely rare to catch malaria in Britain. The mosquito which is capable of transmitting the disease breeds in brackish water near the sea.

While the various insects mentioned are the principal inhabitants of this region, there are also various 'visitors'. In particular, snails and flatworms are commonly seen creeping along the underside of the surface-tension skin when the water is calm. Certain spiders also venture out from the water's edge in search of prey.

In the mud

The only freshwater environments free from mud are fast streams and the wave-washed margins of lakes, where the movement of the water prevents it from settling. In still and slow-flowing water, the bottom invariably consists of mud, and this is the special home of all sorts of creatures.

What is this mud? Partly, it consists of tiny mineral particles — sand, silt and clay. These are washed into the water from surrounding soil, or are blown in as dust. A large proportion of the mud consists of dead remains of plants and animals in various stages of decomposition. This decomposition does not just happen: it is being brought about by seething masses of bacteria, fungi and microscopic animals. This microscopic life is another vital component of the mud, and includes the microscopic plants known as algae which often give a greenish tinge to the surface layers.

Mud is a rich source of food for those animals able to live in it. Many of them swallow large quantities of it and digest the microscopic animals and plants, as well as some of the rotting dead remains. As in most

other environments, these 'grazing' animals are preyed upon by larger carnivores.

The ability to burrow is one typical feature of most creatures found here. Another is the ability to breathe when surrounded by this clogging substance, where there is often a shortage of oxygen. This is a classic example of the way living creatures are always adapted to the environment where they live.

Mud-dwelling animals will invariably be found during the examination of water plants, because a fair amount of mud is pulled up with the roots. But if deliberate examinations are to be made, it is best to scoop up the surface layer of the mud because this is where there is most life. There is more oxygen here and more food in the form of algae (which need light).

The most noticeable inhabitants are the abundant midge larvae or chironomids. Most of them are under 1 cm long, some are bright blood-red, and they swim with an unmistakable lashing, wriggling motion when disturbed. Their worm-like shape is ideal for burrowing and they spend much of their time under the surface of the

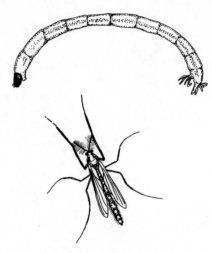

Midge: larva (*top*) and adult

mud. Some species live in silky tubes on the surface of stones or submerged twigs. These tiny tubes, with fine mud adhering to them, can often be seen on the sides of water tanks and goldfish ponds.

Midge larvae feed on organic matter and microscopic life in the mud. They are so abundant that they themselves form a major part of the diet of fresh-water fish. The larger red species are the 'bloodworms' often used as bait by coarse fishermen. The red types are most common where the mud is thick and black and oxygen is scarce. Their colour is due to a substance similar to the haemoglobin of our own blood which enables them to absorb enough oxygen even when it is very scarce. Each midge larva eventually turns into a pupa which resembles the adult, with a swollen thorax and traces of folded legs and wings. The pupa swims to the surface, where it sheds its skin and flies away as an adult.

These are non-biting midges. The evil, biting midges are far smaller, less than 2 mm long. They also have aquatic larvae, about 4 mm long and very slender.

True worms may be distinguished from the wormlike midge larvae by their greater length and the absence of the tuft of filaments that a midge larva has at its rear end. They are referred to as 'segmented worms' to distinguish them from the 'roundworms' which may also be seen. (Roundworms have smooth bodies not divided up into segments, and move with a lot of writhing and lashing.)

The earthworm is a familiar segmented worm and many of the aquatic forms look rather like slender miniature earthworms. Masses of thin red tubifex worms (see page 107) may be found on the mud surface, waving their bodies in a concerted effort to increase their oxygen supply. Tubifex worms are a useful food for aquariums.

One group of segmented worms that has given up burrowing and become adapted to a very different way of life is the leeches, no longer true inhabitants of the mud.

Freshwater mussels and cockles are 'bivalve molluscs', relatives of the snails but having two shells. They live on, and in, the mud, ploughing their way through it by means of the single muscular foot which they protrude from between their shells. When the animal is undisturbed, its shells gape apart slightly, and it is possible to see two openings into its fleshy body. Water is constantly pumped in through one of these openings and out of the other. The creature feeds by filtering from the water various microscopic animals and plants swimming and drifting in it, together with any matter stirred up from the mud.

Mayflies have already been described in the section dealing with the inhabitants of the weedbeds. However, certain species of mayfly larvae may also be found in mud samples. These have their front legs flattened for burrowing, but otherwise resemble their cousins amongst the plants, with their three long tails and gill-fringed bodies.

Although comparatively few species are able to live in the mud, those that can meet the special requirements of this habitat are able to multiply profusely, as there is plenty of food there. The mud is seething with life.

Even this invertebrates' paradise has its predators, of course, chief among which is the dragonfly larva. The closely related damsel flies were described in the section on the inhabitants of weedbeds. The dragonfly species vary in form, but generally they are considerably bigger and more sluggish. Another difference is the absence of the three gills at the rear of the abdomen. The dragonfly larva has its own distinctive way of breathing: water is drawn in through the tip of its abdomen, then expelled when the oxygen has been extracted. In this way, the creature is able to produce a jet of water from its backside strong enough to give it jet propulsion.

Any small worm or insect unlucky enough to pass within range of a lurk-

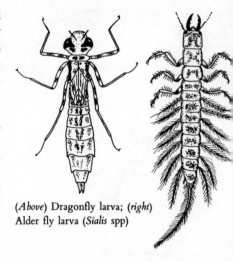

(*Above*) Dragonfly larva; (*right*) Alder fly larva (*Sialis* spp)

ing dragonfly larva disappears in a flash as the extendable jaws whip out and seize it. The beautiful adult dragonfly may be over 10 cm long, depending on the species, and is even more formidable. It is the hawk of the insect world, patrolling a fixed 'beat' of the water margin with a powerful, darting flight, and pouncing on flying insects. A crunching sound can often be heard as it crushes its victim.

The larva of the alder fly also preys on the numerous smaller inhabitants of the mud; its way of life is similar to that of the dragonfly larva. Alder fly larvae can be confusing at first, because they appear to have considerably more than the three pairs of legs expected of all insects. Matters become clearer on close examination, when most of these 'legs' turn out to be long, thin gills fringing the abdomen. (Remember the scarcity of oxygen in this animal's habitat.) The adult alder fly is dark, about an inch long, with transparent, heavily veined wings.

Very small animals and plants

Even a small and relatively inexpensive microscope can open the door to the world of tiny freshwater organisms invisible to the naked eye. Such microscopes are often usefully packaged with slides and instruments, intended for use by children. Many just sit on a shelf and gather dust, as the young owner often lacks guidance on what to use it for. It is a different story when the owner of a microscope has an interest in freshwater life. Some of the creatures revealed make the weirdest science-fiction monsters seem tame, while others are objects of breath-taking grace and beauty. Many tiny plants swim around like torpedoes. There is a constant element of surprise when searching through the most unappealing samples of debris brought home from a ditch.

Most junior microscopes are quite adequate. Try before you buy and avoid flimsy, wobbly models, and those which do not focus easily or tend to slip out of focus. Many microscopes have a rotatable turret bearing a selection of objective lenses of varying powers. To have more than one objective lens is not strictly necessary with an inexpensive instrument; in fact the field of view at higher magnifications may well be very limited in a cheap model. High magnification is no earthly use if you can only see a tiny portion of the creature being looked at. In general, a magnification of x50 is perfectly adequate in a microscope lacking expensive lenses. Separate magnifications are normally marked on the objective lens and the eyepiece. Multiplying these two figures together gives the overall magnification of the microscope. Some microscopes have an adjustable mirror to collect light from an electric

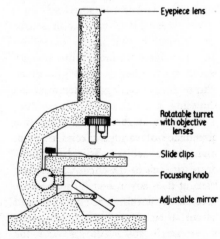

Microscope

bulb or window. Others have a built-in electric light.

A very blurred, distorted image can be produced if you simply dump some wet material on a glass slide for observation. This results from the bending of light, the curved water surface acting as a lens. The solution is to flatten the water on the slide by covering it with an extremely thin glass 'cover slip'. This gives an undistorted image and also reduces the risk of the vulnerable objective lens getting wet. Glass cover slips are extremely fragile and must be cleaned with great care.

To take samples of some algae is a good beginning. These extremely important little plants are, to the unaided eye, perhaps the least appealing of freshwater organisms. Walk slowly along the water's edge, transferring samples to various specimen tubes (or pill containers or small jars) in your pockets. Try to keep each sample separate from the rest. Perhaps into one container will go a waterlogged bit of twig with a haze of greenish-brown slime extending into the water around it. Into another could go a gobbet of bright green slime fished from a green woolly mass covering a patch of mud. Another sample might be taken from the greenish surface of the mud right at the water's edge, and yet another from the bright green, opaque water resting in a cow's hoof-print nearby. Certainly nothing to get excited about so far! Nevertheless, the green or greenish-brown colours were the clues to the presence of algae.

Each sample in turn is prepared for examination. A drop of pondwater is placed on a clean glass slide. A *small* wisp of the sample is placed in this water, using fine forceps or a mounted needle. (A mounted needle can be made by pushing a needle's eye into the eraser end of a pencil.) This tiny sample is then teased out gently across the water drop with two mounted needles.

A cover-slip must be put on to flatten the surface. If this is done carelessly numerous air bubbles trapped underneath will later appear as black circles during examination: avoid this by lowering the cover slip on gently, supporting one end with a mounted needle. If the cover slip now seems to be 'floating', your water drop was too big. If the water has not completely filled the space under the cover slip, the drop was too small. Carefully apply another drop of water to the edge of the cover slip. The flat end of a pencil can be used for this, and the water will quickly be sucked under the cover slip by 'capillarity'.

Set up the microscope with the lowest power (shortest) objective lens, if it has a rotating turret. Looking through the eyepiece, adjust the mirror and/or light source until the illumination is bright and even.

Place the slide on the stage, with the specimen directly under the objective lens. Watching carefully *from the side*, focus the microscope down until the objective lens is very close to the cover slip. If you do not watch from the side, you could crack the slide or, worse, damage the lens.

Now look down the eyepiece and focus slowly upwards until the magnified specimen comes into view. Depending on the sample you took, much of what you now see may consist of grains of sand or silt, magnified like cobblestones, or shapeless masses of decaying plant material. Since the light is coming from below, these will appear dark and opaque. The black circles of trapped bubbles may also be visible. Look out for the green colour of microscopic plants and the movement of microscopic animals. Move the slide slowly with two thumbs as you search.

If you find nothing, waste no more time but make up another slide, perhaps from another of your samples. If you do see something of interest, then you may wish to switch to a more powerful (longer) objective lens by rotating the turret. If the microscope is well made, only a small focussing adjustment will then be necessary. Be careful not to damage the lens against the slide and always focus *upwards* unless watching from the side. Always return to a low magnification when searching for fresh areas of interest on the slide. It makes searching much easier.

If you took your samples carefully as described, looking out for the telltale greenish colour of algae, it will not be long before you are making your first exclamations of wonder at the beauty of these microscopic plants. Perhaps the first you see will be 'filamentous algae'. The many species of this type of algae consist of long, tangled green threads, often

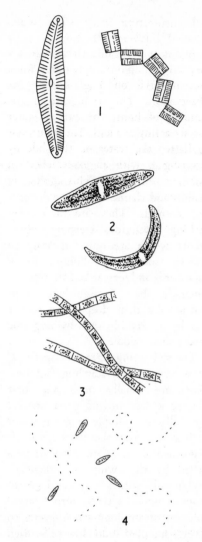

Algae: 1 diatoms, 2 desmids, 3 filamentous algae, 4 flagellates

branching. Under high-power examination each thread is seen to consist of a chain of cells joined end to end, each cell with a complicated internal structure including bright green chloroplasts. Spirogyra is a particularly nauseating green slime when handled, but under the microscope it is the most beautiful of the filamentous algae. Its chloroplasts form delicate and lovely spirals within each of its cells.

Small geometrical shapes, coloured green or brown, will sooner or later be seen: discs, boxes, rods, boat-shapes and crescent moons, some in isolation, others joined together in groups and chains. These are diatoms and desmids. They are often seen making mysterious creeping movements which are quite uncanny to watch, sometimes sliding slowly backwards and forwards. Desmids can generally be distinguished from diatoms by their deep green colour and by a very obvious dividing line across their middle.

The swimming algae, or flagellates, have even more startling abilities. They are usually small and first noticed as fast moving green specks, especially in a sample of green water such as that from the waterside hoof-print mentioned before. They are propelled by tiny whips or 'flagella', visible only with a very good microscope. Some species form larger colonies of anything from several to several hundred individual cells, each with its lashing flagella. *Volvox* is the largest of these swimming colonies of microscopic plants, often filling an area of water with pinhead-sized green specks.

There is endless scope for exploring the world of algae, and it can be done at home on the table after a visit to the waterside. At the same time,

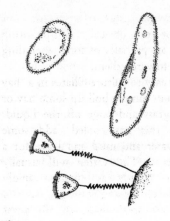

Ciliates

remember the vital importance of these algae. They are the main origin of the 'food chains' in any body of water.

Microscopic animals will always be found, not only in samples of algae but in almost any surface mud or decaying plant material. They differ from the plants in containing no green chlorophyll, and so have to feed rather than manufacture their food like the plants can.

The first microscopic animals you notice are likely to be ciliates. These tend to be small (but not always), colourless and fast moving. Their body surface is covered with numerous short 'whips' called cilia which propel them along. They often rotate as they swim and cross the field of view of the microscope very quickly. If you have sufficient ciliates in a sample, you can often slow them down enough for high-power observation by teasing out a fragment of cotton wool in the water drop before adding the cover slip. Some ciliates are stalked and attached to filamentous algae or other objects. Their pulsating cilia waft particles of food, including algae, towards them.

It is easy to culture ciliates in a 'hay infusion'. Simply boil up some hay or dried grass and pour off the liquid. When this has cooled, add some pondwater and mud and leave for a few days. The water will usually become cloudy as ciliates rapidly reproduce, feeding on the bacteria which are breaking down substances from the hay.

Several species of *Amoeba* may be encountered occasionally. Familiar to anyone who has studied biology at school, this creature is not a ciliate. It moves by 'flowing' rather like an animated blob of glue.

Rotifers might be mistaken for very large ciliates at first glance. They do in fact possess cilia, but these are restricted to the front end and used for feeding. In some species these cilia flicker rapidly on the surface of two projections at the front of the body which consequently look exactly as if they are spinning round. This is the reason for their common name of 'wheel animals'. Many rotifers crawl and swim over plants and mud. Others remain attached by their rear end and a few build themselves protective tubes.

Roundworms, surprisingly, are closely related to rotifers. They are tiny worms, usually much less than half a centimetre long. Their bodies are not divided into segments and they move by vigorous lashing and S-shaped writhing.

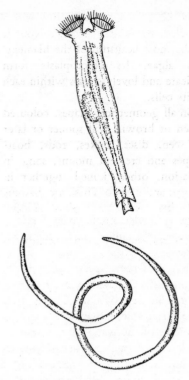

Rotifer (*top*) and roundworm

Larger animals

Small mammals are secretive creatures and the thick waterside vegetation often provides ample cover for large numbers of mice, rats, voles and shrews.

Many of these species may also be found in hedgerows (see Chapter 3, *Hedgerow and Wayside*, page 109), The water vole, however, is a true inhabitant of the water margin. Sooner or later you will see one if you are quiet, swimming at the head of a V-shaped wake. Often a disturbed water vole will plunge in from the bank and swim rapidly underwater out of harm's way, its unwettable fur glistening with a silver film of air.

It is unfortunate that water voles are sometimes called water rats; in fact they bear little resemblance to rats. They do not have the pointed face of a rat and they are big, heavy looking

Water vole (*Arvicola amphibius*)

animals, often up to 20 cm long excluding the tail. They make burrows in the bank, often with an underwater entrance, which explains many a water vole disappearing act; a person may be left scanning the surface and wondering where the vole he alarmed is going to reappear. They feed on plants.

The much smaller water shrew may also be spotted. It is about 8 cm long, excluding the tail, very dark, and has the typical long thin shrew's snout. They are swimming, diving carnivores, feeding on small water animals.

Otters are much less frequently seen, largely because of their intelligence and nocturnal habits. They are not common, but in some areas not as rare as people think. One is more likely to come across their footprints in the mud or even an 'otter slide' down a steep bank where they have been playing.

Waterside birds are a far more familiar sight. Perhaps the moorhen is the most characteristic inhabitant of the marginal undergrowth, and its croaks and squeaks can often be heard when the bird is out of sight. The only similar birds are coots, but these are larger, have a white rather than a red bill, and prefer the open water of larger lakes.

Various species of duck are also certain to be seen. Wild duck have been hunted for centuries and are consequently extremely shy. Some species dive and swim underwater while feeding, while others, such as the common mallard, feed by up-ending themselves in shallow water. The male 'drakes' are more brightly coloured than the better-camouflaged females. The colours are for courtship purposes and when the drakes moult in the autumn they become virtually indistinguishable from the females.

The great crested grebe is a splendid sight in summer, unmistakable with its large, slender form and two-horned head. The behaviour of a courting pair in the spring is a sight worth seeing, and looks like a primitive, ritualised dance.

Grey wagtail (*Motacilla cinerea*)

Small streams have their own bird-life as well. The grey wagtail is anything but grey, with its bluish back, yellow breast and long black-and-white tail. The dipper is likely to take you by surprise as it streaks past with a shrill 'tweet', following the course of the stream. When it alights on a stone it can be seen to be a small, dark bird with a white breast, bobbing

restlessly up and down on its legs. Using the force of the current to hold down its buoyant little body, the dipper walks across the bed of the stream in search of food.

The kingfisher is totally unmistakable and if you are lucky enough to see one you will not quickly forget it. It is very small, all head and beak, but a dazzling orange and blue jewel. It is most likely to be spotted making a rapid flight up or down stream.

The amphibians (frogs, toads and newts) are very closely bound to the water. They have not altered much since the very first four-legged animals crawled out of a prehistoric swamp. When out of water they are restricted to cool, damp places because their thin skin must never dry out. Their ancestors were left behind in the swamps when the first reptiles developed dry, scaly skin and the knack of laying tough eggs on land. So although toads are often found far away from water, they must return to water, along with frogs and newts, to lay their jelly-like strings of eggs every spring.

Newts also venture far from the water after the breeding season is over. They are seldom seen until the following spring, because they are very secretive and emerge to feed mainly at night.

The stickleback is present in most well-established ponds and slow streams. It is quickly recognised from above by its large pair of side fins, the long thin 'wrist' to its tail, and also by a characteristic habit of flexing its body slowly from time to time rather

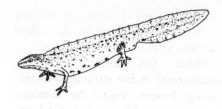

Male smooth newt (*Triturus vulgaris*)

like a cat stretching. Round about May, the males develop their brilliant breeding colours and rival the gaudiest of tropical fish: the back is bluish, the belly a fiery orange and the eyes gleam green as emeralds.

Each male stickleback builds a nest in the spring, using fragments of plant material. Then he coaxes a female to squeeze through the nest and lay her eggs. After he has fertilised them he guards the nest fiercely until the young fish are big enough to fend for themselves.

Sticklebacks will breed freely in captivity, but approximately one square foot of space must be allowed for each male to establish its territory. Even the fat brown female sticklebacks will be driven away before and after the egg-laying stage. It is best to remove females from the aquarium afterwards. Another important requirement to remember is the need for live foods such as waterfleas or chopped worms. Sticklebacks will rarely eat dried fish foods.

Minnows are the fast-water equivalent of the sticklebacks. Shoals of them are found everywhere in rivers, streams and big, stony lakes. When viewed from above, the dark line that runs along the brown body and through the eye is very obvious. They also make attractive and hardy aquarium fish, but obviously require aerated water.

The traditional way to catch minnows is to bash a hole in the funnel-shaped bottom of a clear glass wine bottle, holding the head of a 6 inch nail in place and striking the point with a hammer. Practice makes perfect. The neck is corked and a length of string tied to it. When setting the trap in an area where minnows are shoaling, put in some bread, fill the bottle with water and throw it out from the shore, keeping hold of the string. It is not difficult to catch sixty minnows in one go, so do not take too many. I have found a trap made from a large jam jar even better, using a funnel shaped from perforated-zinc sheeting, held on with elastic bands.

Eels are common in all sorts of freshwater environments. They are all born in the depths of the Sargasso Sea, thousands of miles away. Their leaf-shaped young swim and drift towards the coasts of Europe in the ocean currents known as the Gulf Stream

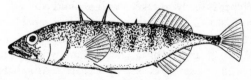

Three-spined stickleback (*Gasterosteus aculeatus*)

and the North Atlantic Current. Their journey takes three years. Many rivers and streams experience an 'elver run' in May, when the young eels arrive at the estuaries and forge their way up stream into freshwater. They now resemble tiny eels about 7–8 cm long and their sheer numbers present quite a spectacle as they struggle up the moss-covered stones at the edges of waterfalls, suffering tremendous casualties from predators. Adult eels too will move overland, especially on wet nights, which explains why they are often found in ponds unconnected with the sea.

Some mature adults return to the sea at the end of the summer, and what happens to them then is unknown.

Other fish might also be encountered in fast streams: speckled young brown trout; the slender, brown loach with its whiskered face; or the ugly bullhead, named after its broad, flat head and enormous mouth.

Most still-water fish will keep well out of your way as you search the shallow margins. But in the spring, you are very likely to encounter the tiny young of the various 'coarse fish' species around weedbeds in shallow water, roach and perch in particular.

Aquariums and freshwater communities

The classic beginners' aquarium is the jam jar, which can be a very useful piece of equipment. Generation after generation of the smallest freshwater animals can be cultured in them. Screw-top jars are essential for carrying specimens home and for use as temporary aquariums to examine specimens at the waterside. However, such jars do not make suitable permanent homes for larger animals, as countless sticklebacks and minnows have found to their cost.

It is a shame that so many freshwater animals perish unnecessarily in jam jars, because most of them are easy to keep at home. The usual cause of failure is overcrowding. If the oxygen in the water is used up, the animals suffocate quickly. If their waste chemicals are allowed to accumulate in the water they may be poisoned slowly. So firstly, the number and size of animals stocked must be in proportion to the size of the container. Secondly, a proportion of the water should be changed periodically; how often depends on how crowded it is.

Jam jars *can* be used. It is possible to make a fascinating miniature 'zoo' of pond animals on a shelf or window ledge, consisting of a dozen or so jam jars with explanatory labels. The typical one-pound jar is suitable for small numbers of small animals, for example two or three freshwater shrimps or half a dozen leeches. Two-pound jars are generally better for anything larger. Big glass sweet jars are useful — ask a shopkeeper. The readily available plastic ones tend to contaminate the water and your freshwater animals may not be appreciative of peppermint or aniseed! Tall containers are not really ideal. Those giving the maximum surface area are best for avoiding suffocation. Various items of kitchen ware may be pressed into service, such as mixing bowls. The largest and most active creatures, for example newts or sticklebacks, should not be kept in anything smaller than a plastic washing-up bowl, and a proper aquarium tank is much more attractive.

Let commonsense dictate how many specimens you place in any container. To keep them healthy, try to err generously on the side of caution. You will find out soon enough if you over-step the limit.

Afterwards, keep *well below* that limit. Only clean containers should be used. The word 'clean' needs explaining. A jar that has been lying around in the garden for years, stained with soil and green algae, is probably 'clean' for the purpose of keeping freshwater animals; a bright and sparkling jar taken from the kitchen sink without rinsing off all traces of detergent could well kill its occupants. Jars that still smell of their original contents should be given a prolonged soak.

Half the water in each jar should be replaced every week or so. Larger containers need attending to less often, unless they are heavily stocked. It is useful to have a bucket of pond water standing by for water changes. Tap water can be used if there is no alternative, but it must be allowed to stand for several days first to get rid of any chlorine. Avoid sudden changes in water temperature.

Feeding will be necessary if specimens are to be kept for more than a few days. Remember that it is easy to kill with kindness. Any excess food left in the water uses up oxygen and forms poisons, whether it is live food or dead and decomposing. Keep a close watch and feed no more than is necessary. Small freshwater animals have very diverse feeding habits, and these make an absorbing study. If proper notes are kept of all observations it is possible for a keen amateur to make important discoveries. Animal behaviour has always been a neglected branch of biology.

The following feeding suggestions may be used as a basis for experimenting.

The water flea *Daphnia* is a useful food for many carnivores. It can usually be obtained easily by regular excursions with the plankton net; alternatively, it can be cultured. *Daphnia* feeds on microscopic algae swimming and drifting in midwater (the 'green-water' algae). Algae require sunlight and water rich in nutrients. This can be arranged by keeping a plastic dustbin full of water in the garden with 6 inches of soil in the bottom. *Daphnia* can be added to the water when it has matured enough for algae to develop. Mosquito larvae will also appear and these are another useful food. They have a characteristic way of scattering down from the surface when you approach.

Daphnia may be fed to the following animals: *Hydra*, water mites, water spiders, phantom larvae and those water boatmen which swim on their backs (the 'true' carnivorous water-boatmen).

Daphnia may also be given to some larger carnivores such as water scorpions, dragonfly and damselfly larvae, alder-fly larvae, *some* water beetles and *some* leeches (experiment). But they may prefer something larger. If mosquito larvae are not available, look for a good concentration of freshwater shrimps or any small aquatic insects.

Although some freshwater animals browse on the water plants with stems and leaves, microscopic algae are far more important as food. The animals likely to feed on masses of the woolly 'filamentous' algae, or on the algae coating plants and stones are these — but bear in mind that each category contains many species whose precise requirements vary: snails, caddis larvae, herbivorous beetles (experiment with *Daphnia* in case your beetles are carnivorous), mayfly larvae, freshwater shrimps and water lice.

Many of the leeches which will not attack *Daphnia* or small insects are likely to feed on snails. Those which suck the blood of larger animals like fish will not be convenient to feed, but are likely to live for months without feeding.

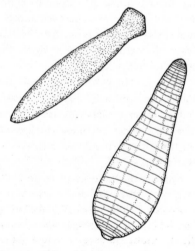

Flatworm (*left*) and leech

Tadpoles and flatworms will feed on small pieces of raw meat and fish. Give very little at a time and remove the surplus. Flatworms are very tolerant of starvation and simply get smaller and smaller. Tadpoles should be released after growing their legs, unless you are confident about being able to supply enough live food for the young adult frogs.

So much for the window-ledge zoo. There is also a less demanding way to keep freshwater life — in a single, balanced aquarium. 'Balanced' means that the various inhabitants, plants, herbivores and carnivores, interact in a more or less natural way so that necessary chemicals in the water are not used up and harmful substances do not accumulate. People who keep fish often talk about a 'balanced' aquarium community consisting of fish, plants and useful micro-organisms, although actually they seldom come close to such an ideal situation, their densely stocked tanks requiring relatively heavy feeding. Much has been made of the fact that plants give off oxygen and use up carbon dioxide produced by animals, so that many people seem to regard their presence as essential for the well-being of aquarium animals. It is forgotten that plants also absorb oxygen and give off carbon dioxide at night, and that dead and damaged plants do this as they decompose. In fact the water surface of the aquarium and any aeration system in use are far more important than plants for the exchange of these gases.

However, it *is* possible to come very close to a balanced, self-sufficient community of pond animals, not requiring much feeding if any — if the aquarium is not overstocked, and if the larger and fiercer carnivores are avoided. Such a set-up can practically look after itself so long as there is plenty of sunlight to support the growth of algae, the primary food of

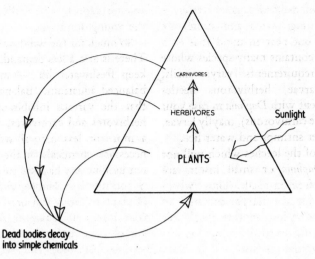

CARNIVORES

HERBIVORES

PLANTS

Sunlight

Dead bodies decay
into simple chemicals

The economics of a freshwater community

any freshwater community. A window-sill is a good location, preferably facing north to avoid direct sunlight.

The aquarium should not be too small; six to twelve gallons is a good size. The unframed glass ones are best, held together with a special adhesive. The small plastic tanks are not all that cheap and easily get scratched. Any aquarium must be placed on a firm, flat base and a sheet of corrugated cardboard or expanded polystyrene will prevent uneven loading and possible cracking of the base.

A quarter of an inch of soil should be spread over the bottom of the tank to help the growth of plants and algae. It should then be covered with an inch of well washed gravel, which is mainly to hold down the roots of water plants and to prevent the soil from clouding the water. A saucer should be placed on top to stop the gravel from being stirred up when the tank is filled. Water from a thriving pond is best because there is no danger of any harmful substances being present. Various suitable species of algae and micro-organisms will also be introduced. Tap water can be used as long as it is left standing for a few days before stocking so that any chlorine can evaporate.

Artificial light will be necessary if the tank does not receive enough daylight. Light bulbs give out a lot of heat so fluorescent strips are better. Algae will be visible after a few weeks. The woolly 'filamentous' algae can be fished out from time to time before the water plants are suffocated. Growths on the front of the tank can be wiped off occasionally, but can be left to grow on the remaining three sides. Dark blue-green algae indicate the presence of too much rotting organic matter — time to change the water completely and clean out the tank.

Cuttings of water plants usually take root quickly and all sorts of small creatures will be noticed in the tank after a few bunches of plants have been pushed into the gravel. Other animals can be added occasionally following collecting trips to the waterside. Some will die, some will survive, many will be eaten. Something like a natural balance will be maintained, provided that the larger predators are avoided.

The regular addition of a wide range of specimens maintains the interest of the display. In such a small 'pond' as your aquarium, many species will inevitably be wiped out completely by predators, leaving you with only a small selection of different species. To compensate for this rule of ecology, inescapable for small-habitats, simply dump a wide assortment of specimens into the tank as often as possible. They will sort themselves out remarkably well. The vast populations of tiny micro-organisms in the community will easily take care of any immediate deaths so long as you do not overdo it. In the process, nutrient chemicals will be released into the water that will support further plant growth.

The diagram on page 101 shows the relationship between plants (including algae), herbivores, carnivores and micro-organisms in any balanced environment. It is a relationship which applies not only to freshwater life but to virtually every environment on earth. Notice the 'pyramid' in the diagram. This illustrates another vital rule — that, weight for weight, there is always a greater quantity of herbivores than carnivores in a particular environment, and also a greater quantity of plant material than of herbivores. Compare the amounts of plant material and of plant-eating animals in your aquarium. Also, if the animal community has had time to become balanced, you will see far more plant-eaters than animal-eaters. (Think also of a field: how much grass and other plants, how many mice, how many hawks?)

The reason for this rule is simply that not all the plant material eaten by herbivores is converted into snail, for instance, or caddis larva or water louse. Most of it is 'burnt up' to supply the animals with the energy they need. Similarly, only a fraction of the animal matter eaten by carnivores is converted into beetle, dragonfly larva or stickleback.

It is essential to bear this principle in mind when stocking the aquarium. Always add far more herbivores than carnivores and, above all, make sure there is plenty of light to encourage the growth of algae, on which everything in the freshwater community ultimately depends.

Collecting with a purpose

Your first aim when visiting ponds and streams with home-made collecting equipment is to explore as many different habitats as possible. It will be some time before all the creatures mentioned in this book have been found. However, there is a danger that as you become familiar with the commonest species you may cease to find them interesting. This simply means that you have not started to observe their way of life in detail. It is not possible to learn much about an animal simply by glancing at it and smugly repeating its name. There is even a limit to what you can easily find out by consulting books. The 'window-ledge zoo' consisting of rows of jam jars and other containers is the best way to find out more. For example, reference books may describe minute differences in appearance between two closely related species of water beetle; you might well discover for yourself that there are very considerable differences in behaviour, preferred food or in breeding habits. Discoveries of that kind can be made by anyone with a little curiosity.

Once the main inhabitants of your local pond or stream have been identified, it should be possible to work out a 'food-web' diagram, showing how they depend on one another for food.

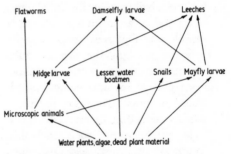

Highly simplified food web for a small ditch community

A detailed knowledge is necessary of what each species is eating. Books may help, but observations on distribution when collecting, and on behaviour in captivity, will be very important. It is easier to make use of such observations if they are written down carefully with all relevant details (and any details that just *might* be important). Observations should be recorded in your notes in an orderly way, not just jotted down at random; a loose-leaf binder is useful. Being scientific is not just a matter of

103

using the correct long words although many scientists do not realise this! It is no more than taking a careful and systematic approach to gathering information. Anyone with a little sense and patience can do that, with or without the scientific vocabulary.

If you have a microscope, never be without a couple of specimen tubes in your pocket. The microscope will continue to reveal surprises long after you are familiar with the commonest of the water creatures that are big enough to see.

After a few collecting trips it will become obvious that the inhabitants of a pond or a stream are not evenly spread out. Different species live in different parts of the habitat. Such information can be set out on a home-made plan of the area being studied. There is much scope for ingenuity when conducting an accurate small-scale survey with such makeshift equipment as a measuring tape, spirit level and lengths of string. Show water depths on the plan, also the position of weed beds (what species?) and any areas shaded by trees (indicate the direction of true north). Other relevant information such as areas trampled by cattle should also be shown.

The next stage is to measure the abundance of various species in each part of the habitat. This has to be done for each of the chosen species in turn. It does not matter if the method used is different for each species, because they are for comparison only. For example you could find out the average number of caddis-larva cases per 10 cm square on the stones along a stream, or estimate the number of great pond snails per square metre in the various parts of a pond, including both weedy and muddy areas. A variety of sampling methods will be needed to make realistic estimates for different species.

One way to present the results would be to make a few copies of the plan, then to write numbers all over each copy indicating the relative abundance of a particular species in different places. Accompanying notes should explain clearly how the numbers were obtained and what they stand for (eg 'Estimated individuals per 10 cm square' or 'Average number of individuals per sweep of handnet after five sweeps').

This sort of study should not extend over more than a week or two because dramatic changes normally happen to populations through the year. These changes are also of great interest and can be studied in various ways. One way is to take a small patch of weed or a single section of a stream, measure the numbers of the commonest species in a given area and repeat this test at intervals through the year; graphs can be drawn showing how their abundance varies month by month.

Alternatively, a single species could be investigated over a year. Evidence of winter migration into deeper water might be found, and it might be possible to follow a yearly life cycle. Young individuals can often be seen growing steadily through the summer, then disappearing in the winter after laying eggs. The average size of animals could be determined at intervals, or the relative numbers of larvae and maturing pupae of such animals as the blackfly might be recorded through the year.

All animals are adapted to their way of life. There are few clearer ways of seeing this principle than by comparing related animals from still and running water. Mayfly larvae are one useful example, those from running water being generally flattened in shape to increase their resistance to being swept away. By studying these and other examples in captivity, many differences can be seen between specimens from such contrasting habitats. Features to examine would be general behaviour, tolerance of low oxygen levels, size of gills, body shape, method of feeding, manner in which adult insect emerges from pupa.

A particularly useful project might be to find out if a suspected source of pollution is in fact causing any measurable harm. Suppose water from a sewage-treatment plant, an industrial estate or a farmyard is draining into a larger stream. Careful estimates should be made of the population densities of various species at points upstream and downstream of the incoming water. Any major differences may indicate that all is not well. The sudden disappearance of stonefly larvae or freshwater shrimps would suggest a drop in oxygen level. A reduction in the numbers of snails and flatworms might be due to poisoning by dissolved heavy metals. A complete absence of animals and

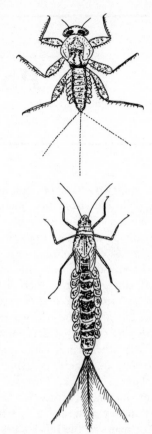

Fast-water mayfly larva (*top*) and slow-water mayfly larva

plants would probably be caused by rotting organic matter if algae and brownish-grey 'sewage fungus' are present. If even these are absent, some serious kind of water poisoning must be involved. Check the situation carefully upstream of the incoming water, for comparison. The surveys should be done in the warmer months when freshwater life is most abundant. The local Water Authority ought to be interested in any carefully gathered data of this kind.

Pollution

There are two ways of looking at water pollution: from the viewpoint of freshwater organisms, or from the viewpoint of man. For example, the drinking water supplied to cities is often heavily dosed with chlorine to kill off any germs or other disease-producing organisms. Few freshwater animals can survive in such water. As far as *they* are concerned, it is polluted.

On the other hand, certain rivers and streams are slightly contaminated with human sewage. Provided the amount does not become too great, this is merely a welcome source of food for many of the inhabitants and does no harm. However, the risk of contracting typhoid fever and other diseases is likely to be high for any human drinking the water. Such water is only polluted from *our* point of view.

Civilised man has lost much of his ancient resistance to disease, and nowadays only clear mountain streams remote from any possible source of sewage are considered fit for drinking, before proper treatment. However there is no health risk at all in studying freshwater life provided that there is not so much sewage in the water that visible signs of pollution are obvious, and that we are not drinking the water. In this section we are more interested in the effects of pollution on freshwater life. Man can take care of himself for the time being.

Sewage *can* harm freshwater life, but in a rather indirect way. The sewage is a rich source of food, especially for all sorts of microscopic creatures. Things get out of hand when too much of it is present. Huge populations of micro-organisms then appear and sometimes use up nearly all the oxygen in the water. It is lack of oxygen that kills off most freshwater animals, not poisoning.

The same effect is produced by any substance that rots — that is to say, any substance that is fed on by micro-organisms. Water draining from an area where a farmer is storing silage is particularly bad in this respect. So are certain types of industrial waste, such as that produced by paper mills.

Streams badly affected in this way are a sorry sight. There are no submerged water plants because these are also suffocated. Slimy masses of algae are the only plants able to

106

survive. Long wisps of greyish-brown 'sewage fungus' on the bottom wave from side to side in the current. These unpleasant growths consist of the various fungi, bacteria and protozoa which feed on the rotting substances and which are tolerant of low oxygen levels.

Some distance downstream from the source of pollution, the organic matter causing the trouble is more or less used up by the organisms feeding on it. Now the oxygen level begins to rise again; the 'sewage fungus' disappears and the first signs of animal life become noticeable again. Tubifex worms, midge larvae and water lice are among the first to be seen. Further still downstream the oxygen level may well have returned to normal with no trace of the pollution remaining.

Even without the use of expensive oxygen-measuring equipment, it is often possible to tell if a stream is slightly polluted. 'Indicator species' such as freshwater shrimps and stonefly larvae need water with a lot of oxygen. If they are absent from streams which otherwise look ideal for them you can begin to suspect pollution of this kind.

Such pollution does not have effects that are permanent, although it may be many years before a cleaned-up habitat is recolonised by the full range of species that previously lived there. Such deoxygenation is basically a *natural* kind of pollution. It tends to occur in small ponds wherever dead leaves accumulate or cattle go to drink, and has been happening for millions of years.

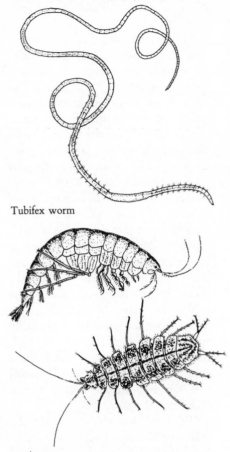

Tubifex worm

Freshwater shrimp (*Gammarus* spp) (*top*) and water louse (*Asellus* spp)

The use of modern chemical fertilisers has resulted in a rather similar kind of pollution, as water drains off farmland. The difference is that these are substances that specifically promote the growth of plants, rather than 'sewage fungus'. Heavy growths of fast-growing algae may choke other plants or turn the water green. A lethal fall in oxygen level is likely when the algae dies and rots at

107

the end of the summer or for any other reason.

Apart from such 'indirect' pollution, there are many substances which do actually poison water creatures. Such pollution is widespread, but often more selective than the kind which removes oxygen. For example, the absence of flatworms and snails from certain streams near old mine workings is the result of poisoning by small quantities of dissolved heavy metals. Insects seem to be less affected by this. Although only part of the freshwater community is affected, this sort of pollution is just as disturbing as deoxygenation because heavy metals are normally removed from the water by various organisms at only a very slow rate. Worse, they are 'cumulative poisons' which gradually build up in the bodies of such creatures as water birds before their eventual death. An affected animal will also pass on the poison to any other animal that eats it.

Old mine workings are not the only source of dissolved heavy metals; these are also present in the industrial wastes that enter our rivers. Many other poisons too are produced by industry, and again many of them are cumulative poisons that can be passed on to predators eating affected animals. To the small ponds and streams that we are considering, the greatest danger of this form of poisoning comes from the insecticides farmers spread on their crops. These tend to be washed into the nearest stream and many of them do not decay but continue to harm populations of living creatures in ways that are often hard to study.

Other substances entering the water harm the inhabitants but not by poisoning. Water draining from certain mines and quarries may contain so many fine suspended particles that plants cannot get enough light to grow. In this way the primary source of food can be cut off, resulting in a barren habitat. The same particles may also clog the gills of some creatures, or completely smother and bury others. The same results can be caused by trampling cattle in a small pond or by boats in a shallow boating lake, stirring up the mud.

I recall a boating lake in a Liverpool park that developed crystal-clear water and a luxuriant growth of water plants when the rowing boats were taken out for overhaul one summer. By the time the boats came back the plant roots had stabilised the mud, preventing the boats from stirring it up, so the water stayed clear and the plants kept on growing. When the weedbeds reached the surface, however, the park authorities received complaints from anglers and treated the water with a fairly harmless weedkiller. The plants rotted quickly in the warm weather, using up a lot of oxygen in the process. Many fish died. A few weeks later the boats were stirring up the mud again and everything was murky normality.

It is a wonder that freshwater life still survives. Yet it certainly does: indeed, it is flourishing and any new, man-made habitats are colonised with astonishing speed.

108

3
HEDGEROW AND
WAYSIDE

Hedgerows are one of the main features of the British countryside, and an attractive one we have come to take for granted. Their variety, the quality and quantity of their trees, shrubs and smaller plants, give lushness and interest to the landscape; for many wild creatures they are invaluable habitats, providing essential food, shelter, or both, not easily found elsewhere today.

Hedges of course are man-made, but their history goes back to the Stone Age, about 4000 BC, when the first people who can be called farmers cleared areas of woodland, established settlements and made ditch-surrounded enclosures for their goats, sheep and cattle. On top of the earth banks thrown up when the ditches were dug they added stockades of wooden stakes, sometimes lashing to them branches from nearby thorn trees, to make them more difficult for animals to penetrate. Thus the use of shrubs and trees for this purpose was established.

Through the Middle Ages and up to the seventeenth century, farming was usually a communal procedure, a large piece of land being cleared, often surrounded with a hedgerow, and divided into strips, each worked by its owner. As the open field method gradually changed, and especially when landowners began to enclose what had been common land, hundreds of miles of hedges were planted — the result being the patchwork landscape that we know today.

Hawthorn (*Crataegus monogyna*)

Double rows of hawthorn seedlings were used for most of the early hedgerows — hawthorn became an impenetrable barrier with regular trimming, and also it was easily propagated and

109

grew quickly; hence its former name of 'quickset' or 'quickthorn'. Over the years other shrubs would grow up among it, and good shelter for livestock, crops and wildlife would build up.

A dictionary definition of a hedgerow is 'a fence formed of living trees or shrubs; a line of bushes, shrubs or small trees, usually hawthorn, privet, yew, etc, planted close, and trimmed level in height and cut back on both sides, so as to form a continuous fence or boundary, especially of a field or garden.' This is the usual idea of a hedge, whether the ornamental hedge planted for privacy in the front or back garden, the one bordering the side of a road, or those criss-crossing and dividing farmland. But there are many different forms.

The so-called 'wild' hedge bordering a lane or track is now usually a mixture of shrubs, sometimes with small trees and climbing plants. Through the survival of the fittest they combine to form the hedgerow. It may run rampant or be cut back on sides and top by the landowner, or by the authority responsible for the lane, when it begins to extend too far. The trees in it may be cut level or be cut around so they grow on in their natural shape. In this 'wild' hedgerow the trees may be there because they invaded it, perhaps from a nearby woodland, as seeds that germinated or as suckers from nearby trees. Elms, for example, throw up numerous suckers.

Other hedgerows began in this way and then were taken in hand by the landowner, shrubs and trees that will

Common English elm (*Ulmus procera*)

not form a thick hedge being removed and suitable species being planted in their place. When there are species growing in the hedgerow that are not to be found wild in the nearby countryside this is the likely reason.

A hedgerow may now be all that survives of a former woodland that bordered the wayside. Much of our woodland has been felled and cleared, as the land has been wanted for crops or grazing. Clues to this having taken place are the plants in the hedgerow bottom. The presence of bluebells, wood anemones, yellow dead-nettle, wood sorrel and other woodland plants, sometimes primroses, indicates that woodland was cleared and the smaller trees and shrubs at its edge were kept as a hedgerow; new growth infilled it and people rapidly forgot the woodland was ever there.

Again, some of the present hedgerows are relics of small plantations of deliberately planted trees. Invading wild trees were sometimes allowed to grow and mature to provide timber, either to sell or to use

110

on the estate for fencing, gates, etc. The trees and undergrowth also acted as a windbreak between two fields or grazing pastures. This sort of hedge-row may be treble the usual width or even more; it may be parallel to the lane, wayside or field, or have a section that juts out into the field as a square or oblong piece of hedgerow before resuming the usual form. Local or county dialect names were given to this type of hedgerow. In Kent, for example, 'carvet' is still used to describe a thick hedgerow or roadside copse; a 'shave' is a small fieldside copse or woodland, while a 'shaw' is a narrow plantation dividing two fields or a copse.

A narrow hedge, either 'wild' or deliberately planted, is often used to border a drainage ditch dug to take surface water from a thoroughfare or field. The hedgerow marks where the ditch is; it may be growing at the level of the adjoining land, or on top of the earth dug out for the ditch.

The hedgerow's form also depends on the landscape it is in, on local weather conditions, or the cultivation taking place and what it is required to do.

In Cornwall, Devon and Wales the 'hedgerow' may really be a bank of earth and rocks, specially laid as a facing, several feet high, bordering thoroughfares and intersecting fields and pastures. On the upper sides and top of the earth bank is a dense growth of blackthorn, hawthorn, furze, bramble or a mixture, perhaps with the occasional small tree in exposed areas; its stunted branches lean away from the dominant wind. All this is higher than the average person and affords shelter to the passerby or to livestock and crops in the enclosed fields or pastures. In Ireland, Wales and Scotland, rock may be used within banks of turf to strengthen it and slabs of rock used upright on the top of the bank. Plants and small shrubs establish themselves in front and between them. This differs greatly from a hedge in southern England, which may grow in richly fertile conditions as a surround to a ploughed field or pasture and consist of trimmed hawthorn or blackthorn, sometimes with holly or beech.

In a county such as Lincolnshire, where the cultivated land is in vast fields, the hedgerow may be a mere hawthorn strip lower than some of

Blackthorn (*Prunus spinosa*)

111

the plants alongside it. In Kent a hedgerow can be 12 feet tall or more, consisting of hawthorn trees which through generations of trimming and topping form a tight boundary and windbreak. Occasional enormous hedges can be seen: one is the famous beech hedge at Meikleour, Perthshire, which is 80 feet high and a third of a mile long.

The contents of the hedge, its trees, shrubs, flowering plants, animals, birds and insects, will vary of course according to their location. A hedgerow close to or bordering a woodland will have a flora and fauna different from the hedgerow on an exposed hilltop, in a grazing pasture, water-meadow or marsh near the sea. A hedgerow of fairly widely spaced shrubs will have less species than a tightly growing protective hedge.

The age of the hedgerow also affects the numbers of inhabitants. A centuries-old, well-established hedgerow will have been used by generations of creatures and plants. Many of them took to it when their original woodland homes were cleared, and ever since have found it a miniature nature sanctuary.

The age of a hedge can be calculated very roughly by counting the number of different species of shrubs and trees (not seedlings and smaller plants) growing along a measured 30-yard length, and allowing 100 years per species. Regional factors such as soil, climate and local hedge-management methods may of course affect your result, but generally speaking it has proved to be accurate within 100–200

years. If possible try to find documentary evidence to back up your findings: the local reference library or the county archivist's department may have maps, deeds or other documents recording dates of boundary changes or changes in land use.

As in the other habitats described in this series, in the hedgerow and country roadside an intricate web of life is balanced. The foliage of the various trees, bushes and smaller plants feeds the young stages, the larvae or caterpillars, of many insects; the dead leaf litter at the bottom of the hedge nourishes the plant growth and shelters other small creatures such as spiders, beetles and snails. All these in turn are food for certain birds; other birds eat the berries and seeds the hedge plants provide — berry-bearing shrubs such as hawthorn in fact crop more heavily in a hedge than when growing in a woodland edge where they are overshadowed by taller trees.

Some of the birds finding food in the hedge are also attracted by its density and build their nests there too, or roost there; larger birds, such as owls or magpies, a passing sparrow-hawk, or predatory mammals such as stoats, will feed on small birds or their eggs and young. Kestrels pick up voles from verges; voles burrow in the soft earth of hedge bottom and feed on slugs and insects there; the slugs live on the vegatation. Rabbits, foxes and hedgehogs may make hidden homes for themselves. The hedgerow is a small world, each animal and plant depending on the others.

If the hedgerow is removed, the consequences for its inhabitants may be disastrous. The hedgerow-bottom soil with its leaf litter and debris will be ploughed in as part of the larger field; it is lost to the wild life. Many species there cannot move what would seem to them a great distance to the nearest similar hedgerow. Some animals and birds may be able to do so, but for the smaller creatures, the caterpillars of butterflies and moths, the ground beetles and so on, the plant species, especially those that need the permanently shady side of the hedgerow, it will mean certain extinction; and their disappearance diminishes the food supply for the others.

Hedgerow removal also has side-effects. Vipers, for example, hibernate in a hedgebottom in wintertime, especially where there is a dry bank and a tangle of tree roots; and the bank may be used as a lying-out place to absorb the sun's warmth in spring, after emerging from hibernation. Snakes may move to a nearby overgrown wayside or a scrubland waste for summer quarters, using the network of hedgerows as sheltered routes; other animals and birds too, if they need to leave one copse or woodland for another, will if possible follow the course of a hedgerow between the two sites, being much safer from predators on their journey. Acting as wind and snow breaks, hedges provide valuable shelter for crops and livestock. They slow evaporation from crops and reduce erosion of topsoil. In some of the English grain-producing areas in Lincolnshire and East Anglia, hedgerows stood in the way of using large farm machinery, but the result of their removal has been that the wind has blown away for ever the vital top soil in this open prairie-style landscape. Hedgerows also act as cover for game birds and habitats for wild bees needed to assist in pollinating clover, fruit trees and other crops.

The total mileage of hedgerow in Britain today is thought to be around 500,000, but going down fast. Several years ago the Nature Conservancy estimated that between 7,000 and 14,000 miles are removed *every year.* The main reason is the economics of modern farming. Smaller fields are sometimes awkward for large agricultural machinery, so the dividing hedgerows are removed to make one large field. Farmers sometimes consider hedgerows a stronghold for 'vermin', pests and weeds. Conservationists, on the other hand, say that the bird and animal life that depends on the hedgerow, apart from rats and mice, does little harm to cultivated crops and feeds on insect pests. Only three 'weeds', they claim, invade agricultural land from hedgerows — thistles, nettles and docks. And some species now live only in hedgerows; if the hedgerow goes, then the species disappears from the area.

But hedge maintenance is ever more costly, and it is now difficult to obtain skilled men to 'lay' the hedge in the traditional way. Without control the hedgerow becomes unmanageable, open and useless for its intended purpose, so farmers replace it with barbed wire or other fencing. Hedgerow and verge maintenance is costly for parish and rural councils, too. With busy traffic, even on narrow country roads, overhanging hedgerows can be a hazard, causing blind corners; so if the road is 'improved' the hedgerow is removed.

Hedgerows are also sometimes killed or badly damaged by careless spraying of nearby crops with chemicals which drift in the wind on to the foliage, or by herbicides used on road verges. They are burnt by stubble fires getting out of control.

But there are signs of public concern over the speed and extent of hedgerow destruction. Various research surveys have been carried out to discover more about what is happening. County nature trusts are using volunteers to restore or maintain old and interesting hedgerows. A few local authorities are also taking enough interest to avoid mechanical cutting of unusual rare shrubs and plants in a hedgerow, employing someone to do the job by hand. The Countryside Committees of some of the county councils and farmers' organisations sponsor hedge-laying competitions and courses to improve the standard of hedge laying and maintenance.

Mechanical hedge-cutters leave torn and splintered branches that would make the old-time hedgeman turn in his grave. Their speed, however, has reprieved many roadside hedgerows; without them, there is no doubt that thousands more miles of hedgerows would by now have been removed, for convenience and economy.

Trees and shrubs

John Evelyn, the famous seventeenth-century diarist, was also an arboriculturist who promoted the creation of hedgerows 'for the benefit and use of future generations'. For a quick hedge he recommended the hawthorn, because 'it provides a dense barrier of spiny twigs and its shape is easily kept in control'. After one year's growth he suggested that timber trees, such as ash, oak, beech or even fruit trees, should be planted at intervals in the hedgerow; two alternatives he advocated were dense blackthorn, which does not make quite such a 'tight' hedgerow, and elder, 'as every part of the tree is useful'. He also hoped to see 'the preciouser sorts of thorn and robust evergreen used more plentifully among the cornel and spindle and hips to make the hedgerow of a spiny hardihood'.

Hedge makers today would not necessarily agree with all he said, but estate owners and farmers in his lifetime benefited; they listened and they planted miles of hedgerows and plantation to make our countryside the patchwork panorama we enjoy. His words may well be behind some

of the beautiful timber trees still seen in some old hedgerows — walnut, maple, oak, ash, fully developed in their natural shape, mature or nearly so, and never, or hardly ever, trimmed.

In the same hedgerow may be some of their offspring, saplings which have grown from seeds, fruit or suckers. Sometimes saplings have sprung up from the stump when a tree has been felled. This frequently happens with ash, elm and sweet chestnut.

The third part of the hedgerow mix are trees which now look like shrubs. When a tree sapling grows through the hedgerow shrubs and its main stem is cut back to the height of the remainder of the hedgerow, it then shoots out in all directions and with regular retrimming stays bushy.

Ash was formerly commonly grown in hedgerows when a tough elastic timber was required for making tool-handles, wheels and even hoops for barrels. It is common on limestone soils, and its pale grey bark, squat black buds and leaves with four to seven pairs of toothed leaflets make it quickly recognisable, summer or

117

winter. The buds are stout and the twigs thick due to the size of the leaves they support. Hedges often include some late shoots that have new dark purple leaves in summer. Mature ash trees produce thousands of winged seeds, known as 'keys'; most do not germinate, being consumed by seed-eating birds and animals. The ash is not a good tree for the hedgerow as its greedy, deep-penetrating rootstock starves other shrubs of minerals and water, so that they die back around it and make a gap.

Common or English elm has been the dominant hedgerow tree of the English Midlands and some of the South West; it was often planted at intervals in hawthorn hedges and, with its towering trunk and massive crown of branches it has become a traditional part of the English country scene. In Kent and East Anglia the smooth-leaved elm is more common. The winged seed is not usually fertile and the tree reproduces itself from numerous suckers around the trunk and from root-branches in the ground a considerable distance from the tree. These have to be cut out from a field, but in a hedgerow they help to maintain its density. An advantage of elm is that because of its height its billowing branches do not over-shadow adjoining meadows and damage crop growth as other massive trees may do — although the branch wood is weak and twigs brittle, so they frequently create a litter on the ground. The double-toothed dark green leaves appear in early April in

Ash (*Fraxinus excelsior*)

hedges, turning yellow, then gold, in late autumn.

In recent years Dutch elm disease, caused by a fungus carried by a beetle that feeds in the bark of dead or dying branches, has decimated the population of English elm trees, and left sad gaps in the hedgerows.

The **common beech** produces a magnificent umbrella of leaves that does cast shade over a field or wayside edge, restricting the growth of crops or nearby hedgerow. Yet this shade equally protects the soil from over-evaporation of moisture and when the leaves fall and rot they mulch and feed the soil. The beech will thrive on poor soil, and endures dry summers and severe winters. When it is planted and

118

kept trimmed as a low hedge its twigs retain their dry brown leaves through the winter and act as a sheltering windbreak, as on the margins of Exmoor. The mature beech tree, with its massive smooth silvery trunk and huge dome of great branches, has a system of strong, spreading roots both above the soil and deep into it, so that sometimes you will see a huge beech with exposed roots that seems to be clinging precariously to the side of a hedgebank. In springtime the soft hairy leaves are pale green; in autumn a golden-brown that seems to set the beechwoods alight. The three-sided brown nuts, the 'mast', are enclosed inside a bristly case. Squirrels, mice and deer, tits and several other birds eat them eagerly, and the size of the mast crop can be vital to the survival of many of these creatures in winter. In the past it was fed to pigs.

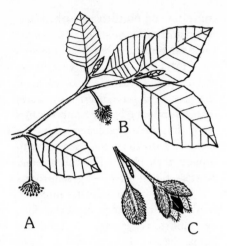

Beech (*Fagus sylvatica*)
(A) male flower
(B) female flower
(C) beechmast and case

Hazel is noticed on many a family walk, due to its hanging yellow 'lambs' tails', the male catkins, in late winter and its nuts in autumn. In the hedgerow it is commonest in the mixed hedges of the South West, Wales and the South East, along with other species such as maple and wayfaring tree, and not so common where most hedges are of planted hawthorn. It will remain a shrub if regularly cut back, but in open wayside becomes a tree up to 30 feet high. As with other catkin-bearing trees, the abundant pollen is distributed by the wind to the female bud-like flowers, which is why they need to appear early, before the dark green, coarsely hairy leaves

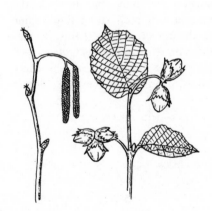

Hazel (*Corylus avellana*)

119

come out and obstruct its path. Hazel wood does not have much commercial value for furniture, but has long been used for gipsy pegs, walking sticks and fencing hurdles; a fork of hazel has been used for centuries by water diviners and long before bamboo canes were imported gardeners cut the suckers, dried them and used them to support their plants. The cob nut and Kentish filbert sold by greengrocers are varieties of hazel; its nuts are relished by birds such as nuthatches, by numerous animals — and by human beings.

Holly is unmistakable, famous as a Christmas decoration. When left to develop it becomes a tree up to 50 feet high, with smooth pale-grey bark. The leathery leaves on the lower portion are spiny, but towards the summit they may have a single spine at the tip or not even this. It was thought the plant had developed prickles to prevent deer and other animals browsing on the lower

Holly (*Ilex aquifolium*)

branches, but now it is thought to be a system of conserving water in the leaves by reducing their surface area. Holly is frequently used as an evergreen hedge, particularly in country house boundaries. When such a hedge has been trimmed for many years it becomes almost solid enough to walk along the top. Holly trees are either male or female, and the white, star-like female flowers must be pollinated from a male tree if they are to bear the scarlet berries. These may remain on the tree until the following spring if the winter is mild, but in hard weather birds will be grateful for them. The white timber, having grown slowly, has a fine grain and is very hard. It is used decoratively in furniture-making and for carving.

Hawthorn is one of our native trees and is common throughout Britain, not only deliberately planted to form hundreds of miles of hedgerows, but also growing as a thick bushy shrub or tree of the wayside. In the counties once extensively farmed on the old 'open field' system, especially in the East Midlands, it was the favourite hedging material when the big fields were divided up, and it remains the predominant hedge shrub. It will rapidly spread out from the hedgerow to invade neglected land and create scrub that changes the character of the area. Birds assist this by consuming the 'haws' and excreting the seeds some distance from the parent tree. Popularly known as the 'may tree', hawthorn was much used for May Day festivities, for decorating exteriors of houses, inns, churches and the maypole itself. Despite the widespread superstition that it is unlucky to take the beautiful creamy-white may blossom indoors, it was hung over doorways to prevent the entry of witches and evil spirits. The thorns are really a form of branch and sometimes are so long they bear leaves. There are two wild varieties in Britain — *Crataegus monogyna* and *Crataegus oxyacantha*, the Midland hawthorn. *C. monogyna* has smaller flowers and its leaves are more deeply indented, the branches are thornier and it is commoner in hedgerows and waysides. *C. oxyacantha* has larger white flowers and is more usually found at the edges of woodlands. Cultivated varieties have rose-pink or scarlet, single or double, flowers.

Blackthorn or **sloe**, related to the damson and plum, earns its name from the black bark on its main stem and twigs that makes a striking contrast to the welcome clusters of white, starlike flowers on the leafless twigs in March and April. If the weather was still severe when they appeared, country people said it was 'a blackthorn winter'. From the flowers the bitterly sour fleshy black fruit, or sloe, develops; it is sometimes made into wine — or sloe gin. The elliptical leaves were formerly dried to make a sort of tea. Whether in a hedgerow or growing separately, the blackthorn is rigid, with numerous tough branches turning in all directions armed with tough, sharp-tipped thorns. It often forms entire hedgerows or is mixed

with hawthorn and other shrubs; also it will escape from a hedgerow and colonise derelict wayside.

Elder was sometimes planted as a hedgerow when a quick screen was wanted, but though a fast grower it would not make a stockproof hedge. Now it is usually seen as an ungainly, sprawling shrub in a hedgerow or as a many-branched small tree of the wayside. Its trunk and branches have a rough, corrugated corky bark, the green shoots quickly hardening into brown wood with a pith core that becomes hollow in old branches. The tiny white flowers are borne in flat-topped, dense clusters; they can be used for flavouring preserves or wine. The later dark purple-black berries are good for making wine, too. The leaves emit a noxious odour not to

Elder (*Sambucus nigra*)

121

everyone's liking, and bunches of them were hung in cottage windows to keep out flies.

Privet is easily recognised, so common is it as a garden hedge, able to withstand frequent trimming. When regularly cut back it bears green leaves through the winter; if a privet shrub is not given this treatment, many of the leaves fall in autumn and it bears exposed twigs with half-open shoots until springtime. The truly wild privet in a hedgerow or wayside has much narrower leaves than the cultivated sort. The single tubelike creamy-white flowers are formed in clusters, and the large purple-black berries are poisonous.

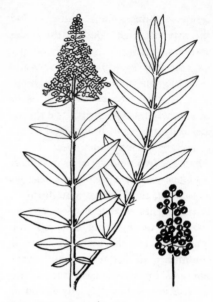

Privet (*Ligustrum vulgare*)

Gorse (or furze or whin) is an untidy evergreen shrub of some hedgerow banks or waysides, especially in heathy areas. Its inhospitable spiny foliage looks as if it would keep out virtually any man or beast; in fact, though, birds welcome it as a safe nesting site. The common gorse's large masses of showy, scented golden-yellow pealike flowers may be seen at any time of year, but especially in April to June; the smaller dwarf gorse flowers later. At first the tiny furze shrub has soft, hairy, trefoil leaves, but as it develops these are modified into spines. The larger spines are also the branches from which the flowers appear. They protect the plant against browsing animals and also prevent excessive loss of water through reducing the area of leaf surface; furze usually grows in

Gorse (*Ulex europaeus*)

122

exposed and heathy places with dry, shallow or stony soil. The flowers develop into hairy seed pods and on a hot day will burst with an easily heard crack, suddenly curling and flinging away the brown pealike seeds; furze soon ousts rival plants and colonises a site.

The **sycamore** or 'great maple' is not a native tree but was so widely introduced to our parks and woodlands in past centuries that it has become thoroughly naturalised. Both tall trees and regularly cut-down stumps, bursting with quantities of shoots, are common in our hedges. Where the sycamore has been allowed to grow, it can be a splendid tree with a dense, domed crown. The lobed leaves, however, are often spoiled by spots of black fungus. The yellowish flowers, hanging in bunches, are not particularly conspicuous, but on a biggish tree later in the year you cannot fail to see the bunches of paired, winged fruits. These are the seeds so often given to schoolchildren to draw as examples of fruits distributed by the wind!

The **field maple** is a genuinely British tree. It is smaller than the sycamore but closely related to it, and common in hedges except in the north. It may be found as a tree or trimmed down. The leaves are the same kind of lobed, palmate shape as the sycamore's, but smaller and with blunt, untoothed lobes; they are hairy underneath, as are the twigs, whereas the sycamore's are hairless. Maple

fruits are also hairy, and their wings are straight and aligned, not angled as in the sycamore.

Wayfaring tree is to be seen by the wayfarer in hedgerows on chalky soils in the south of England. It will reach 20 metres high when unrestricted but is usually a mere 2 to 5 metres, growing best in dry places. The stems, leafless in winter, are never of tree proportions; the shoots are supple, slender, paired on the stem, and thickly coated with hairs; the wrinkled leaves being paired, too, and hairy underneath. As on the elder, the small white flowers are grouped together in flat heads, in May and June, succeeded by flattened bead-like red berries, which later turn black. In winter the large leaf buds have no protective bud scales and are covered with hairs to prevent frost damage.

The **spindle** tree is the straggly small tree or bush that has those brilliant pink fruits in autumn, which split open to show the bright orange-coated seeds. The smooth grey bark and small, elliptical leaves are less noticeable, but in areas with chalky or limestone soil this shrub is often an integral part of a hedge, untidy grower though it may be. Its hard wood was formerly used for spindles for spinning wool and for meat skewers.

Flowers, ferns and fungi

Like a well-planned garden a hedgerow or wayside has a continuance of flowering plants through the year, although obviously there are many more in the spring and summer months. Ferns, fungi and other forms of vegetation are also to be found.

About 600 different plants have been listed growing in hedgerows and waysides. The majority also occur in other places, such as woods or fields, so it is difficult to list 'typical hedgerow or wayside species', but there are many which are commonly found there. They may be using other plants, by climbing up them to the top of the hedgerow; they may grow at the hedgerow base, on the bank, or in a hedgerow or wayside ditch.

Hedgerows and waysides often offer plants several factors they need to thrive. Where they are left undisturbed during their growing and flowering period, perhaps being cut down once at the end of this, in late autumn or winter, they are able to produce seeds for next year's new plants or build up a store of food in their root system. If they have done the latter, some plants can burst into new growth almost before winter's

end. Mechanical trimming of hedgerow verges may hinder their progress, but it may be done after the earlier-flowering plants have grown and seeded, and if done in high summer it allows plants time for further growth and seeding. Also the trimmer may only cut back the foliage of the verge and lower hedgebank near the road and not touch the plants higher up in the hedgerow.

Plants in a hedgerow are to a certain extent protected from low temperatures and the severe weather and winds that would knock them down in exposed places. The dampness of a hedgerow bottom is vital to some types of plants; tall, shady hedges have a humidity that plants such as black bryony require. Open hedgerows are required by wild roses and others with weak stems that need to lean on supporting stems.

Like trees and shrubs, flowering plants prefer particular types of soil. For this reason the flowers found in a hedgerow and wayside can vary widely in different counties; limestone has a rich flora generally, acid, peaty soils a more restricted one. Some plants tolerate almost any conditions.

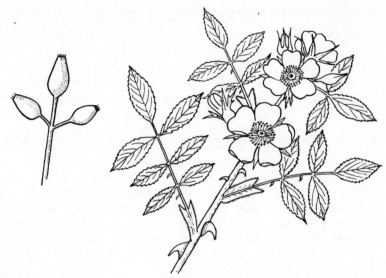

Dog rose (*Rosa canina*)

Dog rose, the largest British wild rose, and the commonest except in Scotland, uses the straight or hooked thorns on its stems to prop itself against neighbouring shrubs, its long branches climbing through the hedge. Its leaves are divided into 5–7 toothed leaflets. On open wayside or waste places it becomes a tall tangled bush. The pulpy section of the so-called 'hip' that ripens in autumn is really the swollen calyx part of the flower, the true fruits, hairy and nutlike, being inside it. Dog-rose hips are pitcher-shaped, which distinguishes them from other roses, on which the hips are rounded.

Ivy, the evergreen climber and trailer, uses the large numbers of adhesive rootlike claspers on its stems to secure itself to its host. As it winds its way up a hedgerow or wayside tree it

often produces a huge mass of foliage and becomes a shrub, almost a tree, in itself, its thick stem nearly hiding the tree. It does not feed vulture-like on its host, as is often thought, but

Ivy (*Hedera helix*)

125

manufactures its own food through its leaves and ground roots as other plants do. If the host tree dies it may be because the ivy has starved it of light and water. When the main stem of the ivy clinging to the tree is cut through the ivy will die. Ivy leaves vary in shape, most often being either the five-lobed shape found on non-flowering shoots, or the pointed heart-shaped type found on bushy flowering branches. The clusters of yellowish-green flowers appearing late, in October and November, are much sought by insects for the nectar and are often abuzz with flies, wasps, beetles and butterflies. The resulting black berries, though poisonous to man, are a valuable late-winter reserve food for birds such as wood pigeons, after the frosts have softened them. Some ivy never climbs but creeps along the hedgerow bottom and woodland floor and also never bears flowers.

Honeysuckle climbs up the side and to the top of the hedgerow by twining its long woody stem clockwise, from left to right, around the stems of neighbouring stronger plants. It may get up into hedgerow trees, or trail along and flop over the top of the hedge. The heads of long trumpet-shaped flowers, cream to buff, tinted with pink or red, protrude in all directions; in the evenings their strong, sweet odour lures passing long-tongued moths to pollinate them. The egg-shaped leaves, dropped in winter, are produed in opposite pairs on the stems. The clusters of bright shiny crimson berries, though eaten by birds, are poisonous to us. Bullfinches raid the berries to extract the seeds, the berry pulp being dropped to the ground where song thrushes and blackbirds consume it. A country name for the plant is woodbine, used also in places for the white convolvulus or bindweed.

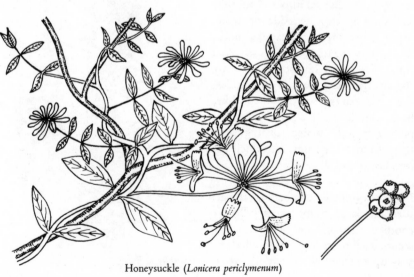

Honeysuckle (*Lonicera periclymenum*)

Black bryony (related to the yam) also climbs clockwise through a hedgerow. The long stems bear pointed, alternately growing, large, shiny, heart-shaped, dark green leaves on long stalks. These are conspicuous in many hedgerows in southern England. The small greenish flowers grow in loose spikes in May and June, and the clusters of soft scarlet berries are attractive in autumn and winter when the leaves and stems have become contrasting bronze or died back and dried out, but are poisonous to man. The plant survives the winter, the swollen fleshy root tubers 'hibernating' deep in the ground out of reach of penetrating frost. The roots are black on the outside, hence its name.

Black bryony (*Tamus communis*)

White bryony, in the cucumber family, is unrelated to black bryony, flowering May to September. The lovely green leaves are ivy-shaped, with five lobes; another difference is that the long stems haul themselves upwards in hedgerows by using tendrils that coil spirally around neighbouring twigs and plants. The flowers are greenish, dark-veined, and the small clusters of poisonous berries change from green to yellow, orange and finally bright scarlet in winter. The fleshy white root-tubers also 'hibernate' deep in the soil, then are able to send up shoots very rapidly in springtime.

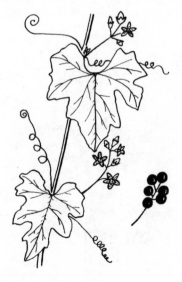

White bryony (*Bryonia dioica*)

127

Bramble (*Rubus fruticosus*)

Bramble or **blackberry** is another hedgerow scrambler and also often colonises large areas of wayside and waste land with its shrublike clumps; where its arching branches touch the earth they put down roots and a new plant grows, which in turn does the same thing. It also climbs, by using

Woody nightshade (*Solanum dulcamara*)

the hooky thorns on its thick stems and the backs of the leaves, familiar enough to all who gather ripe blackberries for jam or wine. Although popularly known as a berry the fruit is really made up of soft, fleshy, juicy drupes, each of which contains a seed. Birds eat the blackberries, fly elsewhere and excrete the seeds, which germinate where they fall on the earth and so the bramble spreads even further afield. The handsome pink or white flowers, attractive to butterflies, come out in June. There are several hundred varieties and hybrids.

Woody nightshade, or bittersweet, is far commoner than its infamous relative, deadly nightshade. It has weak, straggling downy stems several feet long which lean on stronger neighbours in the hedgerow and wayside, often clambering among brambles; dampish places suit it best. It is related to the potato and has similar-shaped flowers which have purple petals and yellow anthers forming a central tube. It flowers June to September. The very dark green leaves, stalked, are in two shapes: those lower down are often three-lobed, with one large and two smaller lobes; the upper stem leaves are spearshaped. The fruits, egg-shaped berries which ripen from green to red, are poisonous, despite the country name 'bittersweet'.

(*opposite*) Woodland hedge, with the tall spike of a foxglove, formerly sought for the heart drug digitalis. Among the ferns the flowers of red campion can be seen (*John Beach/Wildlife Picture Agency*)

Roadside verge, with the yellow flowers of smooth hawk's beard, a relation of the dandelion. Mixed with it are the brown spikes and white flowers of lamb's tongue plantain (*Rodger Jackman/Wildlife Picture Agency*)

Roadside wall with fern in the crevices and lichen on the stones

Typical British field pattern, showing arable land and pasture divided by hedgerow, some containing maturing trees as well as shrubs (*Leslie Jackman/Wildlife Picture Agency*)

This hedgerow has a member of the parsley family (*foreground*) and the yellow flowers of charlock, which likes ploughed soil and survives in the hedgerow when cleared from fields (*John Beach/Wildlife Picture Agency*)

Agrimony is a pretty plant, found in grassy waysides and banks, flowering June to September. Its tall spikes of golden starry flowers on hairy stems give way to small hooked burrs, the fruits, which droop as they ripen and cling to passing animals or humans and thus get distributed elsewhere. The flowers, each of which stays open for three days, were once sought for the yellow dye they yielded, and the plant was used as a cure for liver ailments. The leaves are curious, being composed of seven to nine large, toothed leaflets which have between them several smaller ones on the same leaf stalk.

Agrimony (*Agrimonia eupatoria*)

Herb robert is another pretty but generally overlooked plant of the hedge-bank and waysides. Related to the geraniums or cranesbills, it is an annual, flowering May to October, with spreading, branching, hairy, bright-red stems and deeply divided ferny leaves. The pink flowers have darker red or purple streaks and are normally erect, drooping at night for protection from dew, or, in wet weather, from raindrops. The fruit, when not completely ripe, is pointed like a bird's beak. The plant, especially if trodden on, has a strong smell, which probably reduces its popularity with wild-flower gatherers.

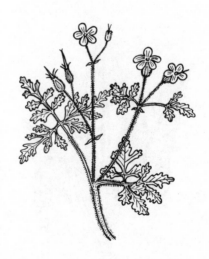

Herb robert (*Geranium robertianum*)

(*opposite*) Prolific vegetation between hedgerow and road, including wild parsley and red campion (*John Beach/Wildlife Picture Agency*)

Groundsel is one of the all-the-year-round flowers, familiar to everyone with a garden. On waysides and in hedgerow bottoms where adjacent land has been recently cultivated, it is a common 'weed', the wind taking the downy seeds to new sites or spreading them around the parent plant. It has some uses though: rabbits enjoy it and birds both wild and caged like the seeds. The leaves are alternate, clasping the stem.

Groundsel (*Senecio vulgaris*)

Cuckoo pint (known as lords and ladies, or wild arum) in the hedgerow bottom may not look like a flowering plant. The male and female flowers are hidden in the bulbous part above the green stem, April to June. Some more undeveloped male flowers are immediately above them around the base of a conspicuous long, club-like purple structure called the spadix; flowers and spadix are backed by a broad pale-green hood, rather like a monk's cowl, called the spathe. The flower emits a foul, urine-like (some say) smell that attracts flies. These crawl down the spathe, past the undeveloped male flowers, past the true male and female flowers and

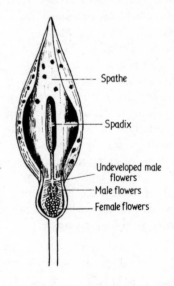

Spathe

Spadix

Undeveloped male flowers

Male flowers

Female flowers

Cuckoo pint (*Arum maculatum*)

134

wander about over the female flowers, pollinating them. The snag for the flies is that when they try to find their way out again the downward-pointing undeveloped hairy male flowers prevent them; they are trapped there until all the female flowers have been pollinated. Then the upper hairy male flowers wither and the flies escape. But they usually go to another cuckoo-pint flower, to go through the same pollination experience again. From the female flowers develop the vivid orange-red poisonous berries, handsomely clustered in a spike. The long-stalked, large leaves are arrowhead-shaped with purple and black spots. The white tubers and roots used to be dug up for their starch, but are now considered poisonous. Cuckoo pint has numerous country names — cow-and-calves, parson-in-the-pulpit, priest's pintle, calf's foot.

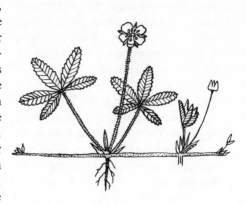

Cinquefoil (*Potentilla reptans*)

Creeping cinquefoil is to be found along the hedgebottom and roadside verge, where it is able to survive the dust and dirt. The yellow flowers, seen from June onwards, look something like long-stalked buttercups although not as cup-shaped; the cinquefoil is closely related to the wild strawberry and belongs to the rose family. From the parent plant, slender stems spread in various directions, sometimes being yards long, at intervals bearing the palmate leaves — the five-toothed leaflets are arranged finger-fashion. Roots grow from the underside of the stems at intervals, to anchor them down, and from these points a new plant grows.

In shady, damp banks and hedgerow waysides some of our most beautiful ferns will flourish. Some of the smaller species like a niche among rocks jutting from the bank or the mossy, decaying stump of a tree.

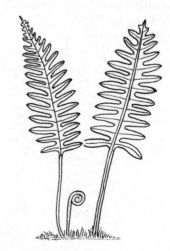

Polypody (*Polypodium vulgare*)

Jack-by-the-hedge, or garlic mustard, is common along shady hedgerows and waysides. Rarely do you find one plant alone; it grows in colonies of sometimes hundreds of plants. It is erect, tall, with fresh-looking heart-shaped, toothed foliage; if rubbed this gives off a strong smell of garlic. The small white flowers are out in spring, followed by cylindrical seedpods. It is related to the wallflowers.

Common polypody occurs among the leaf mould in old hedgerows, or its fleshy roots find a hold in rotting leaves up in the forks of tree branches. The evergreen, leathery, oval-oblong fronds, 18 inches long, are deeply cut into lobes. The better the growing conditions the larger the fronds will be. They are evergreen and when they become well-established their luxuriant growth may adorn the hedgerow bank for years. The brownish-orange spore cases are in rows along the leaflets.

Fungi to be found along hedgerows and waysides are feeding on rotting matter in the soil or upon the decaying tissues of unhealthy or dead trees or shrubs.

Orange-peel fungus is unmistakable in the hedgerow bottom or on the exposed earth of a hedgebank: it looks just like a piece of orange peel thrown on the ground, bright orange on top and paler underneath. Edible, up to 5 inches wide, it is attached to the ground by a tiny stem. In a favourable place several may be growing close together so that it is difficult to distinguish each separately. It is also fragile and cannot be pulled up, breaking into pieces in the fingers. It occurs in late summer, autumn or early winter.

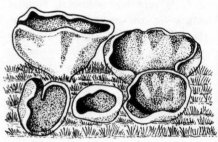

Orange-peel fungus

Birds

Large numbers of different birds fly into and out of hedgerows and waysides. Many are only 'passing through', others live in the hedgerow or nearby, and a few species you are sure to see before long if you watch.

Birds use hedgerows and waysides for various purposes. The hedge is a place to perch while observing the surrounding countryside for food, or enemies, or for others of its own kind if it is a species that lives its life in flocks, or while calling or singing. For some birds it is a good place to obtain food, either on the shrubs or plants or among the debris at the hedgerow bottom or by the wayside, and for these birds the hedge is a convenient place in which to build a nest and raise young. Hedgerows also give shelter to birds, concealment from predators in the air such as hovering birds of prey, and a place to roost at night; owls roost in tall hedgerow trees by day. It is known that many woodland-living birds will adapt to live in the narrower confines of a hedgerow or a wayside with a number of trees if their wood is felled — and most of the birds we think of as hedgerow species in fact adapted to

that habitat when woodland was cleared in the past. This is one reason why hedges are now such a valuable habitat.

If the hedgerow trees are high enough rooks will create a small colony of nests, while a single pair of carrion crows or wood pigeons may nest in a hedgerow with just a few trees. If a tree is hollow and has a hole that can be adapted or enlarged, little owls, barn owls, stock doves or starlings will nest there.

The species of birds and their numbers vary according to the food supply on the trees and shrubs — insects and their larvae, seeds, fruit and berries — and the slugs and snails, worms, and mice and other rodents at the base. For this reason hedgerows that are regularly trimmed and have the bottom cleared out occasionally, or cut back, shelter fewer birds and other creatures than those that are neglected and luxuriantly overgrown. Certain hedgerow and wayside trees, shrubs and plants are hosts to more insects than others. The wayside oak is known to be a source of food to over 500 different insects. A considerable number live on the hazel, but less on the beech and practically none on sweet and horse chestnut.

The **yellowhammer** or **yellow bunting** is a typical top-of-the-hedgerow bird, the male being especially conspicuous with its bright yellow head and underparts, the female is less yellow. It perches on a prominent hedge branch surveying the open country and uttering its unmistakable song, 'a little bit of bread and noooooh cheese'. Yet the nest of grass, moss and stalks, lined with hair obtained in the vicinity, is built near the ground in the bottom of the hedgerow or a shrub. It feeds chiefly on seeds from the hedgerow and adjoining countryside.

The **greenfinch** also sings from a jutting branch but usually higher up, in a tall shrub or upper part of a hedgerow tree, where it also builds its nest. It is the largest of the finches, has a rather solid 'muscular' appearance, and olive-green colouring with bright yellow feathers on the male's wings and tail. It also feeds mainly on seeds but is attracted to a bird table offering peanuts and sunflower seeds.

The **goldfinch** is immediately recognisable, with its bright red face, black cap, white sides to the head and golden-yellow wing-bars. It heralds its arrival in the hedgerow top or on the seeding thistles of the wayside with its cheerful tinkling notes, similar to a canary's. Usually there is a party of goldfinches feeding together, except in the breeding season that

Goldfinch (*Carduelis carduelis*)

starts in May, their dancing flight being another attractive characteristic. The bill is rather more pointed than that of most finches, the goldfinch being thus equipped to extract the seeds deep in teasel or thistle heads. In recent years goldfinches have greatly increased in numbers; they are now protected by law from the cruel and once-common fate of being captured and sold as singing cage-birds.

The **treecreeper** may be one of those 'little brown jobs', but it is easier to identify than most of the small brownish birds that flit around the hedgerows, because of its behaviour — and its long toes, if you are close enough to see them. It looks as much like a mouse as a bird, as it climbs up the trunk of a tree or runs along the underside of a branch, searching for insects and grubs in the bark. Tree-creepers are not often seen in groups, but they do sometimes join flocks of tits and goldcrests in winter. With their whitish underparts and high-pitched burst of song, they may be quite often noticed in hedges with trees, and are particularly interesting to watch.

The **nuthatch** is another smallish bird that runs up treetrunks — or down, or sideways, upside-down or any way — but with jerky movements and much more conspicuously than the treecreeper. Its appearance is quite different too: its chunky, squat shape, blue-grey back and pinky-buff underparts are handsome and distinctive. Its loud tapping as it opens the acorns and nuts it wedges in crevices often lead you along to look for it. The nuthatch nests in a cavity in a tree, perhaps a knot-hole or an old woodpecker hole, and will reduce the size of the entrance by filling it in with wet mud.

The **tawny owl** (or brown owl) is the largest common British owl, living mainly in well-wooded areas though occasionally right in town. You are most likely to notice it first by its eerie call, 'hooo, hooo, hoo -oo-oo', or the sharp 'kee-wick' that often answers the hoot; you may be lucky enough to see it hunting in broad daylight, looking for small rodents at the base of the hedge or in the verge. It most often roosts in a hollow tree or bush by day, but a roosting owl can sometimes be found by following up a noisy group of smaller birds that seek it out and mob it.

The **chaffinch** is related to the former two finches and in areas with

Chaffinch (*Fringilla coelebs*)

plenty of trees and bushes, including either rural or town gardens with hedgerows, it is often the commonest bird. In winter it joins large flocks of other finches. The male has a slate-blue crown and nape, black forehead, red back, green rump and pinkish underparts. During its undulating flight from place to place, the white bars on the wings and white patches on the outer tail feathers are conspicuous, the male's colouring being generally brighter than the female's. When living close to man it can become quite tame, and its distinctive repeated 'pink pink' call note identifies it immediately. It builds a beautiful cup-shaped nest low down in hedgerows, bushes and small trees, using grass, moss and fibres, lines it with feathers, wool and hair and adorns it with lichen, flakes of tree bark and spiders' webs that blend the nest with its surroundings.

The **robin**, a familiar sight in the hedges and shrubberies of parks and gardens, is also a common resident of the rural hedgerow and wayside. The

139

male and female have the same colouring but the young have mottled brown and buff plumage. Universally loved, the Christmas-card symbol of winter festivity, tame enough to fly down picking up insects and grubs around your feet as you work on the garden soil, the robin is far from friendly to its own kind. Each robin has its own territory, an area sufficient in food to support itself and its mate, and woe betide any other robin that ventures into its patch; it will even maim or kill a too-persistent invader. In a breeding season when males are scarce, however, each one may have a 'harem' of several mates in a larger territory, or two mates rather closer together, dividing his time between them. He sings throughout most of the year . . . as a warning to others to stay out. The piping notes of autumn, issuing from deep in a hedgerow on a misty day, have a peculiarly melancholy quality.

The **blackbird** is often the noisiest bird in the hedgerow as you pass near. The presence of a snake or other predator, or the approach of man, often causes the male bird to sound a warning to all and sundry in the area. He retreats into a hedgerow bottom or under a bush, making a chattering alarm, a 'chak-chak' or 'chink-chink'. This is often uttered at roosting time as dusk falls, a dangerous time of day for all perching birds; if a danger gets close he becomes almost hysterical, making a metallic screeching from deep inside the hedgerow. But when singing, often from the vantage point of a tree top or hedge branch, the blackbird is probably Britain's foremost song bird, with loud, rich-toned, flute-like notes and yodelling phrasing. The male is all-black with a bright orange-yellow beak, the female dark brown above, lighter beneath. The blackbird feeds on the ground and frequently nests in hedges.

The **dunnock** is also known as the 'hedge sparrow', but it is not related to the sparrows; it has the needle-sharp bill of an insect-eater. Shy, almost furtive, brown and dark grey in colour, it jerks and hops about among the lower branches or underneath shrubs, and in and around the hedgerow plants, searching for small insects in summer and weed seeds in winter. While doing so the wings and tail are continually flicked. The male overcomes his shyness to sing a warbling song from the top of a low bush to his mate as she incubates their blue eggs in the delicate nest of grass, moss and rootlets, lined with wool, hair and feathers built in the hedgerow or bush. They prefer a nesting site that is evergreen or overgrown with ivy.

Dunnock (*Prunella modularis*)

The **wren** has been known as the mouse bird because of its small size, plumage colour (reddish brown with bar markings) and quick, restless movements as it busies about in the bottom of the hedgerow and on the ground. No mouse, however, has that comical nearly-always-cocked stumpy tail! Using its rapidly moving wings it can sustain flight across wide spaces, as across a road from one hedgerow to another, being seen by the surprised passerby for only a few seconds. It also has a habit of suddenly popping out on to a prominent twig, jerking up and down, then as suddenly disappearing again back in the hedgerow. Another surprise is the trilling song, heard all year, piercingly loud for such a small bird, the call is a loud 'tit-tit-tit' which becomes a churring noise if the wren is alarmed. The dome-shaped nest, with a side entrance, is built in a thick hedgerow, in ivy on a tree or among brambles, and made of moss, grass, leaves, fern fronds, lichen, etc, lined with feathers and hairs. The outside of the nest is camouflaged with material from nearby.

The **blue tit**, also known as the tom tit, blue cap and (in Scotland) blue bonnet, is the acrobat of the hedgerow and wayside. Conspicuous with its bright blue crown, wings and tail, and yellow underparts, it is to be seen high up in the branches of a tree actively searching here and there among the twigs, foliage and bark, first upside-down, then right way up, hanging in almost any position that allows it to snap up a caterpillar, spider, fly or other insect; or it may be low down in a hedgerow bush, rose thicket or bramble clump, again taking prey at an amazing speed. The flight is generally very fast over a short distance between trees or hedgerows. It nests almost anywhere it can find a suitable hole, in a tree, bank or wall, the nest being of moss and grass with a compacted lining of hair, wool and feathers. Incredibly, up to sixteen eggs may be laid in this nest and the tiny young successfully reared, but six to ten is more usual. (The great tit is not only larger but has a blackish head and neck and a black stripe down its front.)

The **whitethroat** is a summer visitor, arriving from Africa in late April to mid-May, departing any time from August to October. It prefers old, neglected hedgerows, field margins or waysides with clumps of furze and beds of nettles. A jaunty little bird with rusty-coloured wings and a long tail with white outer feathers and pinkish underparts, its song is a continual cheerful chatter from the living-place; but if the passerby approaches close to the nest it makes a harsh repeated 'chek, chek' note. A country name for it is the nettle creeper. In fact it builds its nest near the ground among nettles and other plants alongside the hedgerow or bushes, using grass with a lining of finer grasses and hair. Sometimes the female decorates the nest with bits of wool. Like other ground-nesting birds, its eggs or young can fall victim to snakes or rodents; if the male is heard making the repeated warning notes and restlessly flies about in the hedgerow or shrub, it is probably aware that some predator is on the prowl in the area of the nest.

Whitethroat (*Sylvia communis*)

The **blackcap** is a lover of tangled hedgerows, coppices and waste-places where brambles and honeysuckle abound. It is not seen so often as the whitethroat but is immediately recognisable, being sober grey with a black crown or cap (the female's is brown.) It arrives in April as a summer visitor and· sings well into July, when other songsters, with their nestlings to feed, have fallen silent. The song is ended with a flute-like 'hee-ti-weeto-weeto', but the blackcap also steals the notes of other birds and has been known to mimic the nightingale and the garden warbler. The frail nest of dry grass, hair and fibre is built towards the base of a tangly rose or bramble. In recent years numbers of blackcaps have been overwintering in southern England and not leaving Britain in the

autumn. Their diet is mainly insects, but they will also take soft berries like those on ivy.

Two handsome but very different black-and-white birds are often to be seen busying round the hedgerow. The **pied wagtail** is immediately recognised by the constant bobbing up and down of its long tail, black with white outer feathers, as it searches for insects on the ground. It is a familiar sight on waysides near gardens or fields, even in suburban areas.

The **magpie** belongs to the crow family and is a substantial bird, unmistakable in its smart black-and-white plumage as it hops rapidly across a road from hedge to hedge, walks along or chatters harshly from a tree or tall shrub. In sunshine its wings gleam with irridescent blues and greens and its tail has a purplish gloss. Magpie nests, domed and made of sticks, are often plainly visible in tall hedgerow trees. Not particularly nervous of people (or cars), magpies seem to have adjusted well to urban areas where biggish trees can be found. They eat a wide range of food — insects, snails, small rodents and — for which in the past they were persecuted by gamekeepers — the eggs and young of smaller birds, as well as fruit and vegetable matter. They will sometimes bury acorns as a squirrel does.

Related to the magpie, the **rook** can be identified from the carrion crow by a whitish patch around the base of its bill. It is also gregarious, moving about in flocks, whereas the carrion crow remains solitary or in a pair. Where the hedgerow trees are high, rooks will use them for a rookery, particularly if near open fields where there will be a food supply of beetle grubs, worms, leatherjackets, weed and crop seeds. Rooks do take corn and will damage other crops but this is usually outweighed by the pests they take in large numbers. The bulky nest is built of twigs and turf, cemented together with earth and lined with straw, grass, moss, hair and wool — it may be last year's repaired with fresh material or a completely new nest. Rooks will return year after year to the same rookery, then in one nesting season, for some unexplained reason, they will abandon it and choose a new site. It is said that if they build high it will be a fine, calm summer, but if they build lower down it will be a wet, windy summer!

The **kestrel**, our commonest hawk, is an interesting bird to see. It is chestnut brown, the male having a grey head and tail with a black tail band. Formerly it lived on open moorland, hillside, field or marsh. But it has adapted to hovering over the embankments and reservations along our motorways, finding them a refuge for the small rodents on which it feeds. No one tramps about there, and the traffic hurtling past on either side does not worry them. The kestrel has also learnt that changes in agricultural cultivation have forced some of the prey it used to find in the fields into the hedgerow verges. It is also known as a windhover due to its distinctive way of hanging stationary, head to wind, rapidly fanning its long pointed wings to keep itself in position: this is how you are most likely to see it from the car. If it cannot spot anything edible it quickly glides away to another position, repeating the operation again and again, until it finds an unsuspecting rodent or a beetle, on which it swoops with lightning speed by shutting its wings and dropping to earth. It uses the old nest of a crow or magpie, or a hollow tree in a hedge or woodland, a cavity in a ruin, a quarry or cliff face, in which to nest. It is also increasingly coming into towns and cities to hunt the park and garden hedgerows and nest on building ledges.

Mammals and reptiles

You may walk along the length of a hedgerow or wayside and not see a single animal, but that does not mean none are there. As you are moving, they sit tight and stay hidden, waiting for you, an unknown danger, to pass, or they sleep quietly until night time. To see the local animals and other creatures active in daytime, find somewhere secluded, behind a hedgerow tree or in an evergreen bush, even just sitting unobtrusively at the bottom of a stile, and keep still, quiet and watchful.

It may not be too long before you hear leaves being rustled and searched, then see foliage being pushed through or climbed up or over, or movement among the shrub branches or around the bottom of a tree trunk. If you do, remember not to blink; do it slowly if you must — a keen-sighted animal will see the movement of your eyelids and the flash of the whites of your eyes, and will be gone, at least for a while.

You may already have found evidence of animals being in the area. Where rabbits, foxes or badgers regularly pass through the hedgerow bottom they make a gap by pushing aside the vegetation, and the earth either side of this may be trodden hard, perhaps with footprints still visible. There may be other regularly used trackways in the hedgerow bottom.

Another sign is a near-bare patch where pellet-like rabbit droppings are grouped together, or among the debris the corkscrew-like pale brown droppings of a weasel or the dark brown, pointed, slug-like droppings of a hedgehog. Chewed or shredded grass and plant leaves, nibbled acorns, rose hips and hawthorn haws, hazel nuts with a hole in and the kernel gone, teeth marks on fallen crab apples and other wild fruit, sweet chestnuts half-eaten and with the rind stripped off, gnawed pine cones, toadstools with chunks gone from the cap or stem, young twigs with their tender bark gnawed, and the remains of dead birds and animals, of slugs or snails and their broken shells, broken birds' eggs, hair caught on spiny plants and shrubs: all these are evidence that animals are around.

Earth at the bottom of a hedgerow is often looser than in neighbouring land, and if it has a ditch it is also better drained. These two facts, with the protective cover of the hedgerow and close proximity of a regular supply of food, make it an ideal place for animals to burrow and make their summer and winter living accommodation and store place. Here you may find the entrance hole or holes of a rabbit colony, with earth scattered around the entrances. Smaller holes can be the entrance to a vole's or mouse's burrow; only by witnessing the animal using it or by identifying the tracks is it usually possible to identify the owner. A larger hole or holes, especially if a refuse dump of waste food, apples, etc, is heaped near or in the hedgerow, may be the entrance to the common brown rat's burrows.

You may see a young weasel or inexperienced rabbit dash across a road from one hedgerow to another. There may also be sad evidence upon the thoroughfare itself of animals that did not run fast enough. The rush across of a rabbit, vole, shrew, rat, mouse, stoat, weasel, snake or slowworm, the slower perambulation of hedgehog, mole or toad, is so often on our traffic-busy country thoroughfares the final action before the creature's life ends as a flattened corpse.

The **hedgehog** is probably the most run-over animal in Britain and yet its population total shows no sign of declining. It lives not only in hedgerow bottoms, but also in woodlands, ditches, city parks or town gardens. Mainly nocturnal, it emerges at dusk from its daytime hiding place in a heap of leaves or debris to forage for its prey — slugs, snails, beetles, earthworms, insects, mice, rats, frogs, lizards, snakes, berries or, near dwellings, household waste such as bacon rind and meat scraps. It will come out after a heavy rainstorm to snap up the slugs and snails that also emerge. Never kill a hedgehog living in your garden: it consumes a vast number of slugs. In the past people used to keep a hedgehog or two in their kitchen to keep down the cockroaches, but — even if you have cockroaches — this is not advisable as hedgehogs often carry fleas. In the past, gipsies and romanies used to capture and kill hedgehogs, wrap them in a ball of clay and cook them in the hot ashes of a fire. When ready, the clay was broken off and with it came the 'spines' so the flesh could be eaten. I am told it tastes like pork, hence its rural name of hedgepig, but that at certain times of the year it is rather fatty! The male and female 'hedgepig' are called the boar and sow, apt names when one listens to them squeaking and grunting as they prowl around. They also snore while asleep. The 'spines' are really modified hairs which can be raised or lowered at will. Hedgehogs

Hedgehog (*Erinaceus europaeus*)

are strong climbers but if they fall will immediately roll into a ball so that the muscles around the base of the 'spines' take the shock of hitting the ground. Apart from motor vehicles their chief enemies are the fox and badger, but these only attack if acutely hungry. If a hardy fox does try to bite into the prickly ball, the hedgehog emits a noxious smell.

It hibernates in autumn, making a nest of dry leaves, moss and similar debris in a hedgerow bottom or a compost heap, under a pile of cut brushwood (one did so under my garden shed), or even inside an old wasps' nest enlarged and lined with dry materials.

The **weasel,** or its near relative the stoat, will occur wherever there are rabbits and small mammals such as mice to prey on in a hedgerow or wayside. Its short legs and lean, slender body allow it speedily to pursue a victim through the entrance hole and into the burrow to kill it underground. It is an agile climber, seeking birds' nests for young and eggs, it can leap what must seem to it wide distances, and it swims to pursue frogs or water voles or to escape.

Weasel (*Mustela nivalis*)

146

Inquisitive and cunning, if disturbed it may dash into the vegetation, but if the passerby stands still, the weasel's head may soon pop out of its hiding-place, its steely-black eyes surveying the situation. Victims are killed by a bite at the base of the skull.

The weasel closely resembles the stoat, but is smaller and its tail does not have a black tip. It has reddish-brown fur with white underparts and runs with an arched back and a gliding movement. Despite its small size (about 10 inches with a 2 inch tail) it will courageously attack animals larger than itself, even rats that are equally fierce when cornered.

A **common shrew** sometimes gives away its presence in a hedgerow bottom by making high, shrill squeaks, particularly when it meets another shrew. The males are fierce and quarrelsome when confronting each other. Brown and grey in colour, the head and body are about 3 inches with a tail half as much again. Active by day and night, the long sensitive snout that extends beyond its mouth twitches as it continually searches for earthworms, insects, snails and slugs; the shrew has a hyperactive digestion — in 36 hours it consumes four times its own weight and if for some reason, perhaps through being trapped, it cannot obtain food, it starves to death in a very short time. Its bones are frail and though it climbs rapidly a shrew often dies from the impact of a fall. If picked up it can also die of shock. Although able to bury itself in loose earth in 12 seconds when surprised, this is rarely quick enough to prevent it from being seized by cats, hawks, owls, magpies, stoats, weasels or vipers. It spends the winter foraging in the hedgerow bottom and ditch, in summer moving out to the wayside and rough pasture where there is deep grass to shelter it.

Common shrew (*Sorex araneus*)

The related pigmy shrew, Britain's smallest mammal, head and body 2¼ inches long, weight 5 grammes — less than a fifth of an ounce — also occurs in the same places and has similar habits. If you find a dead specimen a clue to its identity is that it has red tips to its teeth.

The **bank vole** inhabits hedgerows and woody landscape. It is bright, chestnut red with whitish underparts and long hairy tail; it measures about 3¾ inches. In daytime all the year round it climbs up among the twigs in search of berries, fruits and seeds, nuts, buds or the bark of young trees and shrubs. Nibbled hips and haws, either still on the plant or lying at the base, or bitten fragments of a toadstool indicate that bank voles are about. They dig up roots and bluebell bulbs, take wheat and barley grain from adjoining fields, take birds' eggs and young, snap up insects. They will kill other rodents and sometimes the quarrelsome males fight to the death, the victor eating the loser! Shallow burrows are made in a grassy hedgerow bank, in a sunny position, with many entrances and exits; the vole can dash down a hole at the bank top and reappear at one lower down some way away.

Bank vole (*Clethrionomys glareolus*)

The **long-tailed field mouse** or **wood mouse** (one and the same animal) commonly occurs in the hedgerow and wayside, where it burrows, and in gardens too. In the latter this attractive little creature can occasionally be a nuisance, digging up newly sown peas and bulbs, damaging or removing strawberries, gooseberries, apples or flower buds: it may also eat berries, grain, acorns, seeds, nuts, snails and insects. When disturbed it runs rapidly and can make prodigious zig-zag leaps to escape. In appearance it is similar to a house mouse, for which it is often mistaken, but it has more reddish-brown fur and

147

Long-tailed field mouse (*Apodemus sylvaticus*)

larger eyes and ears. Head and body are about 3½ inches, with a tail as long again. It is also a prolific breeder, but its numbers are kept under control by the many creatures that prey on it: owls, hawks, stoats, weasels, foxes, hedgehogs and vipers. It is so short-sighted that it can sometimes be quietly approached and captured under a hand.

The **harvest mouse** was originally mainly a cornfield dweller, but the use of the combine harvester drastically reduced its numbers. Survivors took up residence in suitable untrimmed hedgerows adjoining fields. Here they construct their ball-shaped summer homes, 3 inches in diameter, beautifully made of plaited and woven grass blades, among tall grass and vegetation, in bramble shrubs or furze bushes above the ground, instead of as formerly upon several stems of corn; by this adaptation it has not only survived but is beginning to increase. Charming to look at, timid in

Harvest mouse (*Micromys minutus*)

character, the tiny harvest mouse is active in the day, easily climbing up a stalk to sit on an ear of corn or head of cow-parsley seed. Head and body are about 2½ inches, with a tail as long again. The tail (scaly and almost naked) is so pliable that it can be coiled to grip a corn or grass stem almost as an extra foot. It constructs burrows in the hedgerow bottom to store grain for use in winter and here it spends periods asleep. In summer it mainly eats soft leaves and insects, grain, seeds and berries when available.

The **viper** or adder likes to lie in the sun to warm itself and prefers a sunny bank that has a hedgerow with a ditch nearby. It eats mainly shrews, voles and mice so the hedgerow provides it too with its food. Vipers do have a poisonous bite being the only British snake to have this, but they are given an undeservedly bad reputation. If they are poked with a stick or someone attempts to pick them up they will retaliate by biting, but normally they usually move away into the nearest cover, a nettlebed or bramble bush, even bracken, if they detect the vibrations of a human footfall. They are shy, retiring creatures, and in any case their mouth-gape is small, the danger is that they could seize a finger or toe, or the soft flesh of a hand or foot, if someone gathering low flowers such as primroses accidentally touched them. During autumn several vipers may be seen in the same hedgerow bottom, seeking a dry hole in the bank, a disused animal burrow or a hollow under a litter of debris and leaves in which to hibernate during winter. Colour and markings are very variable but there is usually a dark wavy or zig-zag line down the back, with spots and white dots on either side.

Viper (*Vipera berus*)

The **slow worm** is not a worm or a snake, but a harmless legless lizard. Its body is scaled like a snake's, but the anatomy has vestiges of limbs discarded some time during its centuries of evolution; it also has a notched tongue like a lizard, not the snake's forked tongue. It is golden yellow and bronze in colour, and very glossy. Its snake like appearance often leads ignorant people to kill it, but its diet is simply small earthworms, insects and spiders, and certainly no gardener should kill it because it consumes as many slugs as it can find. In spring it likes to doze in the sunshine on a warm hedgebank or in a sunny ditch, unless searching by day for prey in the hedgerow. Later in the year it spends all day in a hedgerow bottom where there are stones under which it can hide, coming out at dusk to feed. In winter it hibernates in an underground burrow or a hollow under a large stone. When alarmed it will dive into loose soil or beneath a stone and speedily vanish. Its main enemies, apart from man, are hedgehogs and vipers.

Another sunlover by the side of a hedgerow is the **common lizard** — not all that common today. It finds a bare patch of earth or a tree stump, and basks upon it, if disturbed shooting forward horizontally into the nearest cover. It moves rapidly over plants with a gliding motion, body and tail hardly lifted off the ground, to seize flies, beetles, moths, spiders and caterpillars; these it swallows whole unless too large, when it chews them for a while. It is difficult to capture, and if you succeed do not hold a lizard by its tail: it can snap this at a weak point and you will be left holding the wriggling end while the owner escapes. It will grow a new tail, shorter and blunter. After a lizard has been disturbed and dashed into the nearest hiding place, it will return to the sunny place when it thinks danger has gone. Lizards are supposed to be responsive to unusual sounds, and loud whistling is claimed to coax them back from hiding!

Slow worm (*Anguis fragilis*)

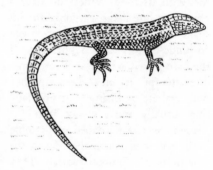

Common lizard (*Lacerta vivipara*)

150

Insects and others

The insects found in and along a hedgerow and wayside are of course those that can find there the protection they require, the trees and plants on which they lay their eggs, the plants or other insects on which they feed. A hedgerow with a wide range of flowering plants and shrubs is going to attract and house a larger number of different insects than one with only a small range of varieties. As with birds, many of the winged insects seen along a hedgerow or a wayside will also travel elsewhere, going to adjoining habitats such as woodland edges or fields. Some regularly occur along the hedgerow and wayside, a few colourful butterflies being particular favourites.

The **orange-tip** butterfly appears in April to June, in dancing flight from flower to flower. The male has the orange patch on the front wings, but the female has only a blackish-grey patch. The underside of the back wings of both male and female is beautifully marked with green mottling which shows through to the upper side. Eggs are laid on jack-by-the-hedge (page 136), where the bluish-green caterpillars, with a white stripe on the side, may be seen.

Orange-tip butterfly (*Anthocharis cardamines*)

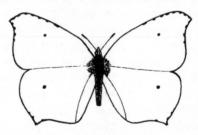

Brimstone butterfly (*Gonepteryx rhamni*)

The **brimstone** butterfly comes out even earlier, being attracted out of hibernation from February onwards if the weather is warmly favourable. The male is sulphur-yellow, the female a paler greenish-yellow; both have a central orange spot on each wing. Eggs are laid on buckthorn, the caterpillars being green in colour with black dots. It is claimed the name 'butterfly' was first used for the brim-

151

stone, which centuries ago was called 'the butter-coloured fly'; the name was later shortened and applied to all 'butterflies'.

The **small tortoiseshell** butterfly is common wherever there are beds of stinging nettles in a hedgerow or wayside. It is reddish orange with yellow patches, black-and-white spots and blue crescents, though markings are very variable. The green eggs are laid in a group on the underside of a nettle leaf in May. From these the black-and-yellow caterpillars emerge to feed as a colony on the nettles, using strands of silk to draw leaves together to form a shelter. When the leaves are consumed right down to their main ribs, the caterpillars establish another communal feeding place, and so on until half-grown; then they separate to feed singly. When there are enough of them the nettles can be stripped, although new shoots eventually grow. The small tortoiseshell is one of the butterflies that fly indoors in autumn, into a shed, barn or house, to find a place to hibernate; they will cling to the folds of a curtain or an old coat, or stay in a cupboard or dark corner for months on end.

Dragonflies are often seen zooming along hedgerow tops and edges and over waysides. These brilliant insects of many colours and patterns are great travellers, with such a speed of flight that they are found far from the lake or pond where they spent the early part of their life cycle in the water, in

Small tortoiseshell butterfly (*Aglais urticae*)

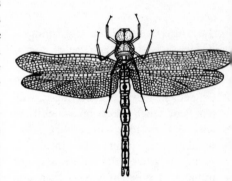

Dragonfly (*Odonata*)

Bumble bee (*Bombus*)

152

the 'nymph' stage. Long before man could do it dragonflies had mastered the act of hovering in flight, even flying backwards. The very large eyes have between 10,000 and 30,000 lenses, depending on the type of dragonfly. A dragonfly cannot focus its eyes as we do, but each lens looks in a different direction and so it can see movement from every angle. It feeds on insects, such as mosquitoes and flies, many of them pests, seizing them in flight, then perching on a twig and holding the victim with its front pair of legs while it severs the wings and pulps the victim's body with its jaws. Dragonflies are still widely believed to sting — they are sometimes known as 'horse stingers' — but they do not even possess any stinging apparatus. A more harmless insect, except to their insect prey, would be hard to find.

A **bumble bee** seen flying in and out of the low plants at the hedgerow bottom is probably a female searching for a suitable hole or disused animal-burrow entrance in which to make a nest. With her jaws she cuts grass blades, moss and bits of hay, which she takes into the hole and there creates a sort of matting. In the centre of it she makes a space, then flies in and out fetching flower pollen and nectar. In the nest centre she puts the pollen on the floor, then moulds it with nectar to make a paste ('bee bread') that she spreads in a circle or plate. On this she lays her eggs, covering them with a wall and roof of wax from special glands on her abdomen.

Using more wax she makes a 'honeypot' about the size of a hazel nut at the entrance to the nest, and puts in it a supply of honey for herself and her brood in bad weather. Then she sits on the wax 'roof', the warmth of her body helping to hatch the eggs. The grubs find a ready supply of food, which she adds to as needed from her honeypot. Within a week the grubs are full-grown; each makes itself a cocoon and changes to a pupa; in another fortnight they become adult bumble bees and fly away. In the meantime the mother bumble bee has made new paste and laid more eggs, so a further generation of adults is raised.

The name really should be humble bee, coming from the German *hummel* bee, referring to their humming noise; but it was thought that the bees 'bumble' along in their heavy flight, so the name bumble bee has stuck. There are many different sorts, some very handsome, some identified by the colour of their hairs on the largest part of the body: red-tailed bumble bee, yellow-tailed bumble bee, buff-tailed bumble bee among others.

The **common wasp** has spoilt many a wayside picnic: it has a remarkable ability to detect sweet substances, your jam sandwiches or sweets being especially attractive, as is flower nectar or ripe and over-ripe fruit — anything with a high sugar content. As the wasp has a narrow mouth, it can only lick up liquid foods. It will, however, grab other insects, such as grasshoppers and similar creatures, paralyse them with a sting, cut off the wings, roll the remaining corpse into a ball, tuck this under its body, grasping it with its legs, then fly off to the nest to feed the victim to its grubs.

Common wasps will not deliberately attack people unless someone starts swatting at them, when they become angry and attempt reprisals. Most stings occur in late summer or autumn when wasps become 'sleepy' and may be touched or trodden on in the house. When a number of wasps are continually flying on to your picnic feast, walk back along both sides of the hedgerow for a considerable distance: if you see wasps frequently coming in and out of a hole in the hedgerow bottom or hedge-bank and returning to it, then that is the site of their nest colony, which may house up to 25,000 wasps in a season! They are not likely to attack if you just stand still watching them, because they are far too busy, but it is unnerving to share your chocolate cake with these seemingly aggressive insects, so beat a retreat to a further part of the hedgerow or wayside. Badgers have no such fears, being equipped with a thick fur coat that angry wasps will not sting through. If you see the torn, grey, paperlike remains of a wasps' nest pulled out of the hedgerow bottom, this is where a badger or two obtained a wasp-grub meal.

The **crab spider** is just one of several spiders common among the hedgerow and wayside vegetation. Others create

Common wasp (*Vespa vulgaris*)

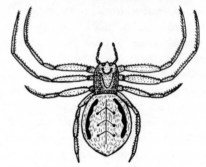

Crab spider (*Misumena calycina*)

the well-known orb cobwebs, complete with trip wires that cause passing insects to fall into the trap. The crab spider, though, does not spin any sort of web. It just waits for a victim to come to it. After climbing a plant or shrub, moving its squat body with a crablike action, it may crawl inside an open flower, such as bramble, pressing itself against the central parts of the flower or the petals to make itself unspiderlike in shape; its first two pairs of long, powerful forelegs outstretched and waiting. When a bee, butterfly or fly alights on the flower, the spider's powerful legs have seized it before it has realised its mistake, and it is soon a corpse being sucked out by the spider. If you see a butterfly or other insect struggling upon a flower a

154

closer look may reveal it is in the grip of a crab spider.

The spider has an amazing ability to change its colour to match its surroundings; it varies from near-white to pink, yellow or green, depending on the flower or foliage where it lurks. If a pink-coloured spider is put on a white or yellow flower, it will change its colour accordingly, then change back to pink if eventually replaced upon a pink flower. The colour change takes a day or more — it does not happen fast enough to watch the whole thing.

The bottom of an overhanging hedgerow, where the sun does not penetrate, is permanently damp. Here, among the debris, leaf litter, decaying plants and dense living vegetation several snail species thrive.

The **white-lipped banded snail** is one of the easiest to recognise. Its yellow shell is boldly marked with brown stripes or bands, so that it looks like an old-fashioned peppermint humbug. Occasionally the yellow shell has fewer bands or none, or the bands may be broken into a series of spots. The snail's body

White-lipped banded snail (*Cepaea nemoralis*)

is greenish-grey with a yellow tip to the tail end, and the opening of the shell has a white lip — hence its name. Its colouration might seem to be inviting discovery by hungry birds, but when the sun shines through the foliage, casting light and shade among the leaves and stems, it is sometimes difficult to see it against a light stem or pale leaf. The snail feeds on grass and various hedgerow plants.

Related to it is the **brown-lipped banded snail**, found more in grassy waysides and woodland edges. As its name indicates, the pink, yellow or brown shell, often with five bands, has a brown lip; the snail's body colour is lead-grey or yellowish-grey. Thrushes enjoy both sorts of snail when they discover them, using some particular stone in the hedgerow bottom, as their 'anvil', on which to smash the shell.

4
THE SEASHORE

The seashore teems with strange and fascinating forms of life. It supports a greater variety of different animals and plants in a small area than almost any other environment on earth. Perhaps only tropical rain forests can match this sort of diversity; and though such places are far away, the truth is that most people could probably name more animals and plants in an African jungle than they could on the nearest seashore.

The scenery and the wildlife of the seashore have changed little since the end of the last ice age: it is our land's last wilderness. This small book is intended as a first introduction to an all-too-unfamiliar world of beauty, colour and endless surprise.

Survival on the shore

That the seashore is a very suitable place for life will be confirmed by a single glance at a sheltered rocky shore or a shovelful of estuary mud. On the other hand a number of special difficulties face all the inhabitants of the shore. Having evolved to contend with these difficulties has made the various seashore species quite different from their close relatives living in the

steadier conditions below low-tide level. It is always instructive to look at any seashore creature and think how its design and way of life qualify it for survival in this rich but dangerous environment. Consider each of the following difficulties in turn . . .

Waves

A shore facing the full fury of a gale is an impressive sight. Big waves break against rocks with pressures of tons for every square foot. Great masses of water move at speeds attained in rivers only below the world's greatest water-falls. All this happens in a normal gale, many times a year. When the storm dies down the rockpools still contain little prawns gingerly picking their way among delicate anemones and seaweeds, and the limpets are still browsing on the rocks.

Large rocks are the only stable element during the chaos of a storm and a number of animal species are designed to cling to them tightly, as do the various seaweeds. The other occupants of a rocky shore are skilled at seeking safety in the relatively calm conditions in crevices or beneath boulders. For animals living on a sandy shore the sole solution is to burrow.

Moving stones
Stones are transformed into underwater bullets during a storm, and there can be little protection against them. This is why loose shingle beaches are uninhabited. So, usually, are rocky outcrops on shingle beaches.

Some animals, such as the various snails, are also likely to become living missiles in rough weather and their shells are much thicker than those of offshore species.

Drying-out
Drying-out means death to most shore animals and plants, although some have become able to tolerate it to a large extent, like the seaweeds found at the very top of the shore. The need to remain damp is another reason for hiding away among rocks, or burrowing. Limpets and mussels have watertight shells, barnacles and winkles have tight-fitting trapdoors. The seaweeds stay moist because of their coating of slime. Many of the animals, including rockpool fish, are able to breathe air for a while, so long as they stay moist.

Temperature variations
Depending on the season, the shore is subject to both scorching heat and freezing cold; the temperature of the sea remains fairly constant. Hiding and burrowing are only partial solutions for shore animals, which have to be more tolerant of extremes of temperature. Winter cold seems to cause most trouble and many species die off then, or move down below low-tide level. The shore comes back to life every spring.

Freshwater
The bodies of sea creatures are adjusted to the fact that seawater contains a lot of salt (a good spoonful in every pint), and that the amount of salt remains constant, except in estuaries; any great variation is very harmful to them. Most small animals from below low-tide level die within seconds of being placed in water with no salt in it. Creatures on the shore, however, are often exposed to diluted seawater when rain falls at low tide. Watertight shells, hiding away and burrowing can all help to shield them, but these animals do have to be tough enough to survive some variation in the saltiness of the water.

Being eaten
Life on the shore is doubly dangerous. At high tide, great numbers of predatory fish and crabs move in after the rich pickings, while at low tide the shore is the hunting ground of flocks of sharp-eyed seabirds. It is no surprise that the animals living here are real experts at camouflage and concealment. Have patience and cunning when searching for seashore animals — it is not only you that they are hiding from.

Tides
It is the rise and fall of the tides that

make the seashore such an interesting place, enabling us to walk over a region which for some of the time is part of the bottom of the sea. The shore is best explored at low tide so a little basic knowledge of tides is important.

The rise and fall of the sea's level is caused by the pull of the sun and moon as they pass across the sky. For our purposes we need say no more.

There are roughly six hours between low tide and high tide. That means there are roughly twelve hours between successive low tides. Low tide (and high tide) are between twenty minutes and eighty minutes later every day. Inexpensive tables can be bought in seaside areas, giving the times of high and low tide every day of the year. The times are usually those for the nearest major port and there will be a list of tidal constants to add or subtract from these times. The tables are easy to use once you know the 'tidal constant' for your area. The timing of the tides varies a lot from place to place, since the shapes of the coast and the seabed affect the flow of the water.

Spring and neap tides
Every fortnight the tide comes in particularly high and goes out particularly low. These are known as spring tides and are especially good times for seashore exploration.

A week after the biggest spring tide comes a time of neap tides, when high tides are not very high and low tides, unfortunately, are not very low. These neap tides also come every fortnight. Once again the tables give useful figures indicating how far out a particular tide can be expected to go.

There are exceptionally big spring tides every March and September, when very low tides enable us to get further down the shore than at any other time. All sorts of particularly interesting creatures are uncovered then.

Rocky shores

In places where the sea meets the solid rock of our land, an ancient battle is continuing. At times, even the hardest rocks have broken under the impact of big waves. A cliff face may only suffer a fall of rock once in a century, and the grinding and smoothing by sand and stones carried in the waves is a slow process. All the same, after many thousands of years of splitting and shaping colossal masses of rock, the sea has gradually formed our familiar coastline of eroded cliffs, smooth boulders, gravel and sand.

Each type of shore has its characteristic population of animals and plants. The smooth rock of a cliff face is often exposed to the full force of storms and offers few hiding places. Only tight-gripping animals like barnacles and limpets are found here and even seaweed growth is limited to a few sparse clumps. Shores with scattered boulders and rocky crevices have plenty of little animals taking advantage of the numerous places to hide from the dangers of the shore. The more sheltered the shore, the greater the variety of animal species present and the greater the amount of seaweed growth.

In some places there are steeply sloping shingle beaches of loose, rounded stones whose continual movement prevents anything from living there. Other shores are composed of finer fragments — fine gravel, sand or mud. Animals can live in comparative safety in these areas by burrowing, and such shores are described in the next chapter.

'Arriving'

One of the characteristic features of seashore animals and plants is their ability to 'arrive' and colonise every available object, from rocks and jetties to a moored dinghy or an old shoe. This is one of the secrets of their success on the shore.

Most seashore animals produce vast numbers of young. These larvae are usually microscopic in size and totally unlike their parents in form. With the aid of fins, paddles or tiny pulsing hairs, they swim and drift in vast numbers along the coast in spring and summer. The assorted young of barnacles, worms, seaweeds and many others are all for a while part of this world of drifting microscopic creatures, known as plankton. They

159

are often carried great distances by currents, feeding and growing until they are ready to settle on the shore. Many are eaten long before this stage is reached, for all sorts of animals in the sea depend on plankton for food. Those that survive rely on the sheer chance of bumping into a suitable surface when they are at the right stage of development. The fortunate ones immediately hang on for dear life and proceed with their growth into the familiar adult forms. Even now their problems are not over, for many will be killed in the next storm, or eaten. (In the early summer, look out for areas of rock covered with thousands of tiny young barnacles or mussels, newly settled. Then go back at the end of the summer and see how few have survived.)

Most creatures that you find on the shore will have had literally millions of brothers and sisters less lucky than themselves. This is how seashore animals are able to colonise every possible home, and why most species produce so many offspring.

There are some exceptions to this pattern. For example some seashore snails lay smaller numbers of eggs, which are safely fastened down or hidden away. These hatch out directly as tiny crawling snails. A much higher proportion survives, but any new areas colonised have to be reached the hard way — by crawling.

Finding rocky shore animals

The variety of rocky shore life is so tremendous that no truthful person dare claim to be able to identify every-thing he finds without referring to a book. When the common animals on pages 163–5 have become sufficiently familiar, there still remains a lot to discover. At that stage, *Collins Pocket Guide to the Sea Shore* is helpful.

Preparation

The first thing is to select your shore, if you have any choice. The rockier the better; the more boulders and crevices the better; and the more sheltered from big waves the better.

Equipment is the next thing. Wellingtons are usually the best footwear. A plastic bucket and a pocketful of polythene bags are as good a way as any of bringing back specimens to look at more closely. A small net is also useful. The cheap nets with thin bamboo handles can be improved by stitching the flimsy wire frame to a piece of wire coathanger, which is then secured to the handle with plastic tape.

Timing is very important as the lower end of the shore is the most interesting, and it is best to start shortly before low tide, preferably a spring tide. The slight effort of consulting tide tables in advance is always repaid.

The hunt

When you arrive on the shore, your initial reaction might well be one of disappointment — perhaps all you can see are seaweed-covered rocks and a few snails. But provided the tide is reasonably low and there are a fair number of boulders and crevices, you can find a lot more. Stoop down and look closely, remembering that many seashore animals are quite small and expert at camouflage. Look carefully into pools, move aside clumps of weed and, best of all, lift up loose rocks. You will immediately begin to make discoveries that elude casual visitors to the shore, and the next hour will pass very quickly.

Lifting rocks
The practice of lifting rocks is a controversial one. It is the most effective way of revealing plenty of animals in their hiding places. However, there are many areas where this has been done on a large scale by anglers collecting bait and by numerous 'educational' excursions. It is common in these places to see overturned rocks everywhere, and the animals and their eggs attached to what was the undersurface of each rock have generally died as a result. Worse, any seaweeds now trapped under the rocks die, and the stinking black mess that results makes those rocks unusable as hiding places for a long time. Half an hour of this unintentional vandalism can ruin a stretch of shore for the rest of the summer, with harmful effects lasting much longer.

There is no need for this to happen. If each rock is carefully replaced as it was found, little harm results from moving it. The few creatures accidentally crushed are quickly replaced by the immense fertility of the sea and they will not have died in vain if some interest in seashore wildlife has been encouraged. Far, far

more damage is done to the seashore as a result of ignorance and indifference, from industrialists, legislators and the public.

Please replace rocks as you find them, and encourage others to do the same.

Headlands
Rocky headlands come alive with nesting seabirds for a short period during the spring. Gulls lay their large, speckled eggs in crude nests everywhere. Some of the other visitors are seldom seen on the shore at other times: these are the birds of the open sea. Guillemots and razorbills sit on cliff ledges, looking like miniature penguins. Their relatives, the puffins, nest in rabbit burrows while fulmars circle in the air like stiff-winged gulls.

The top of a rocky headland is a good place to watch for seals. They often look like swimming dogs when they surface, on their way to hunt fish in the next bay. Watch out as well for the low, graceful, looping jumps of a school of porpoise or the huge, triangular fin of a thirty-foot basking shark. Most impressive of all is the sight of a gannet far out at sea, folding its large, white wings at a height of 200 feet to streak vertically down towards a shoal of mackerel. The water erupts with a tall, thin splash as with the impact of a naval shell.

Winkles are often collected for eating (only on clean shores with no sewers nearby). They are very common snails, usually dark grey or black, of about 2cm. Like the flat winkle and the **rough winkle**, they can breathe air and are protected against drying-out by the round, hard trapdoor at the shell opening, which distinguishes them from the dog whelk.

They feed on seaweed and the microscopic plants which form a green slime on the rocks. Their tracks are often visible meandering across sandy areas, or as dried slime trails on sun-warmed rocks.

The feeding movements of their mouths can be seen if some winkles are put in a glass jar of seawater. They have a tongue like a conveyor belt equipped with rasping teeth.

Flat winkles have rounded tops and are usually found amongst thick growths of seaweed. They can be quite difficult to spot among the air bladders of **bladderwrack** and **knotted wrack**, which they resemble. The dark green individuals are particularly well camouflaged, but nobody seems to have produced a satisfactory explanation for the bright yellow variety which seems to be just as common. One would think these would be more vulnerable to hungry birds. There must be a reason for the beautiful, conspicuous yellow colour of these little shells, but it remains to be discovered.

Rough winkles are smaller and feel rough to touch. They too have colourful shells — yellow, red, white, brown, black, or various banded combinations. They are well adapted

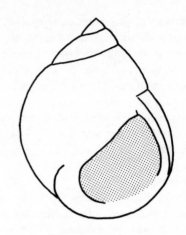

Winkle (*Littorina littorea*)

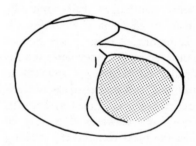

Flat winkle (*Littorina littoralis*)

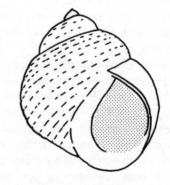

Rough winkle (*Littorina saxatilis*)

for life at the drier top end of the shore, as they can breathe air easily. Like the other types of winkle, they are able to seal the mouth of the shell with a round, horny trapdoor to prevent drying-out. On a hot sunny day with the shells sealed in this way they can remain glued to the rock with dried slime.

Rough winkles do not lay eggs like most snails. Instead the young are incubated inside the pointed end of the shell.

Top shells, with their triangular outline, are more closely related to the **limpet** than to the winkle family. Like the limpet, they have gills which cannot tolerate being clogged with mud, so they are never found in muddy places. They are not as good at breathing air as the winkles, and are only found on the lower half of the shore. A layer of mother of pearl often shows through worn shells.

When top shells are on the move a number of waving tentacles extend in all directions. To make a sluggish top shell move, put it in a rockpool and touch it with a starfish. Watch it move away, tentacles waving frantically.

Dog whelks are carnivores whose mouths have a special arrangement of teeth for drilling through the shells of such animals as the **barnacle** and the **mussel**. It is said that dog whelks feeding on barnacles have white shells, while those feeding on mussels become brown. However it may not be as simple as that, and some

individuals have brown and white bands. They can be distinguished from the winkle by the grooved projection extending from the shell opening.

The clusters of ¼ inch long, straw-coloured, flask-shaped objects fastened to the underside of many stones are the egg capsules of dog whelks. About ten little snails will emerge from each capsule.

Top shells

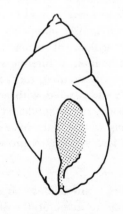

Dog whelk (*Nucella lapillus*)

165

Limpets are snails whose shells are cone-shaped rather than the characteristic spiral and are often overgrown with seaweed or barnacles. They are common on all clean rocky shores and are one of the few species able to withstand the battering of waves on exposed shores and cliff faces. They can cling extremely tightly and, unless taken by surprise, are difficult to dislodge, even with a stone.

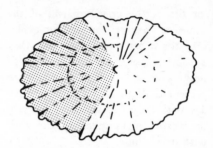

Limpet

Limpets feed on seaweed and there is often a little clearing marking the grazing area of each one. Each limpet returns to its position before low tide. The shell of 3-4cm grows to fit the shape of the rock, and the rock itself may be scarred with the impressions of long-deceased limpets.

Mussels have bluish, double shells held in place by bunches of tough little strings, and they filter their food from the seawater. Plankton, that range of tiny, microscopic animals and plants drifting and swimming in the sea, is eaten by a wide variety of animals, including mussels, which do not have to move around in order to feed. Each mussel pumps something like ten gallons of water per day through its internal filtering system.

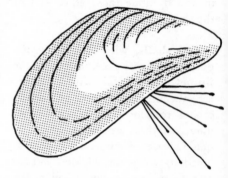

Mussel (*Mytilus edulis*)

In the early summer, rocks in some areas become covered with countless tiny mussels, showing where the free-swimming young ones have settled. Only a few survive to grow much bigger.

Beadlet anemones are non-swimming relatives of the **jellyfish** which can be dark red, brown or dark green. Individuals covered by water in rockpools are usually opened out to 2-3cm, revealing the stinging tentacles around the central mouth. The design is that of a jellyfish turned upside down and stuck to a rock.

Small animals which bump into the tentacles are stung to stop their struggles. The tentacles pass them towards the mouth, which gapes to engulf them.

A ring of bright blue beadlets is often visible around the base of the tentacle region. This is the reason for the name. Many other species of sea anemone may be found, but the beadlet is usually the commonest.

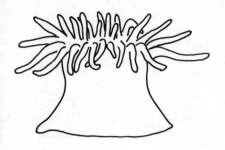

Beadlet anemone (*Actinia equina*)

Barnacles are extremely common, particularly at the upper end of rocky shores. Although their small (under 1cm), whitish, conical shells resemble that of the **limpet**, barnacles have trapdoors at the centre and are actually crustaceans, along with the **shore crab, prawn, sandhopper,** and others with armoured bodies and jointed legs.

The tiny young barnacles swim in the sea before cementing themselves down. A microscope reveals their jointed limbs and clear resemblance to the young of many typical crustaceans.

If you submerge a barnacle-encrusted stone or shell in a rockpool they will soon begin to feed. A bunch of feathery limbs will emerge from each little trap door and rake microscopic animals and plants from the water.

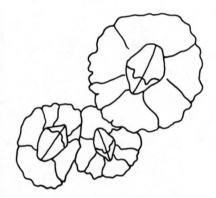

Barnacle

Hermit crabs are active little crabs which lie still when they see you coming, often among numerous empty shells. This trick is effective but it is usually possible to find one, the tips of his claws and legs just visible inside the snail shell he carries on his back.

Their tails are soft, fleshy and coiled to fit the shell and the rear legs are reduced in size, serving only to hold the shell in place. One of the main preoccupations of a hermit crab is to find suitable replacement homes. They measure with their legs each shell they find and move house constantly. Larger shells are needed as the crab grows.

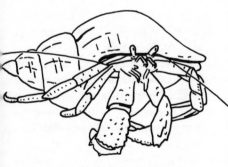

Hermit crab (*Eupagurus bernhardus*)

167

Shore crabs are successful animals, common in every type of seashore environment — rocky shore, sandy shore, muddy estuary and on the seabed below the low-tide mark. They are commonest of all on a rocky shore, hiding under stones and in seaweed at low tide. Their triangular shells vary from green to reddish brown.

Like all other crustaceans, they have to shed their armour periodically in order to grow. Soft and flexible, they emerge through a split at the back of the shell, leaving a perfect hollow ghost behind, complete even to the eyestalks. Meanwhile, the soft, vulnerable crab hides away for a week or so while its new shell hardens, a size bigger than the old one.

Shore crab (*Carcinus maenas*)

Edible crab (*Cancer pagurus*)

Edible crabs, as the name suggests, are the crabs most commonly eaten in Britain. They grow to a large size, with oval shells, reddish-brown colour and black-tipped claws. Good specimens may sometimes be found near the low-tide level. Usually, however, it is the smaller individuals that are seen on the shore, crouching motionless beneath a stone or clump of weed. They seem sluggish and do not struggle much when picked up; but the claws of a large edible crab are even more to be respected than those of a lobster and it is instructive to see what they can do to a wooden pencil or a plastic pen.

Prawns are only pink when cooked. In life, their transparent bodies and careful movements make them quite hard to see. They walk slowly over rocks and seaweed in sheltered pools, picking at all sorts of food with their tiny claws. Occasionally they rise from the bottom and glide through the water, propelled by special limbs under their tails. They have a long jagged spike projecting forward between the eyes.

Just as your hand or net is about to scoop up a prawn you have stalked, there is a flicker and it disappears completely. It has snapped its fanlike tail beneath its body, shot away backwards, and is about a foot away, keeping as still as it can.

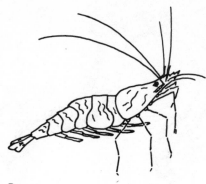

Prawn

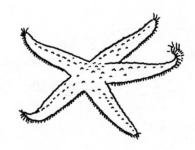

Starfish (*Asterias rubens*)

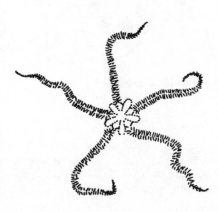

Brittle star

Starfish are usually orange/yellow and have a distinctive way of moving. If you look closely at the underside of a starfish, normally found on the lower shore, you can hardly fail to notice the hundreds of characteristic little tube feet, each with a tiny suction pad at the end, which enables the starfish to glide along. They are hydraulically operated by muscles that squeeze against the water inside each tube foot.

Starfish feed on a variety of animals such as the **barnacle** and the **mussel**. The mouth is underneath and the stomach turns itself inside out through it to digest its prey externally.

Brittle stars are relatives of the **starfish** with very long, flexible arms. Like the starfish, their undersides have numerous tiny tube feet, but brittle stars do not rely on these for moving around. Instead, they drag themselves along rapidly, using four of their whiplash arms in succession. A fifth arm is usually extended in front as a 'feeler'. Their appearance while moving in this way is very strange indeed. After a moment you begin to regard the leading arm as a sort of head and it is most upsetting when the creature decides to make off in a different direction, another arm immediately taking the lead.

Ragworms are often seen if you lift up a stone with sand or gravel under it. Their burrows are visible under such stones and any ragworms exposed will quickly retreat from

169

view, moving like centipedes, using bristly projections on each side of their bodies.

The biggest species, known as the king ragworm, grows up to a couple of feet in length. This type is much sought by anglers for bait. It has black, pincer-like jaws which are capable of drawing blood, so handle with care.

There is a huge variety of worms in the sea. Unlike the humble garden worm, their bodies are often decorated with all sorts of colourful tentacles, bristles and gills.

Ragworm

Blennies, patterned with blotches of dark or light green, are common rocky-shore fish of about 9cm. They are often found under stones at low tide, out of water but perfectly happy. So long as they stay moist they can continue to absorb oxygen from the air until the tide returns. Their large, paired front fins hold them upright and they can 'walk' out of water using these fins and the tail.

Blenny (*Lipophrys pholis*)

One of their favourite foods is barnacles, and their jaws are powerful enough to remove these from rocks with apparent ease. Just try doing it with a fingernail! The large jaw muscles and domed forehead account for the appealing and unfishlike expression on the blenny's face.

Butterfish (*Pholis gunnellus*)

Butterfish, of a similar size, are also found under stones at low tide. They resemble small eels, but have a row of black spots down the back and a separate tail fin. When uncovered, they may lie still at first, hoping to

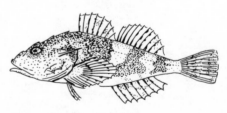

Sea scorpion (*Taurulus bubalis*)

170

escape notice. If disturbed, they become wildly acrobatic, wriggling and flipping until they gain the refuge of another crevice. The first one you manage to catch will almost certainly succeed in squirming between your fingers. They are as slippery as butter and their flanks are butter coloured.

Like the **blenny**, butterfish may be found guarding their eggs in the spring. These are laid in a clump under a stone and are guarded by the parents until they hatch.

The **sea scorpion** has an ugly shape, but can be very colourful. It has a huge mouth and long spines on its gill covers, but the spines are not poisonous (do not confuse with the **weever**) and will not prick the skin if the fish is handled gently. The teeth are very small, so that cavernous mouth will not bite, but this fish is still often persecuted by anglers. Sea scorpions are extremely well-camouflaged and varied in colour. The blotches resemble patches of algae on a rock, and the belly is usually a pale, yellowish green, though bright red individuals are sometimes found.

This species is another example of parental care — in early spring the males guard small masses of eggs in safe hiding places on the shore.

Sandy and muddy shores

Sandy beaches are more familiar to seaside visitors than rocky shores. They are more comfortable to sit on and apparently uninhabited by any of the small seashore animals which, unfortunately, are regarded with suspicion or disgust by the average holidaymaker. There is nothing for seaweeds to fasten to and so sandy beaches appeal to tidy minds. Not least of the attractions are the properties of sand itself, which have fascinated generations of children.

Most seashore pebbles have short lives of only relatively few years before they are smashed and ground away by the waves. Most sand grains are far older. They are the hardest fragments surviving from rocks that were ground away long ago by the sea or by huge glaciers of the ice ages. Look closely at a pinch of sand. On a typical golden-yellow beach most of it will consist of these ancient little particles of hard silica (basically the same substance as glass). Small, younger, fragments of other types of rock may also be present, betrayed by their different colour and size. Often, numerous tiny pieces of broken shell give the sand a whitish colour and

varying amounts of mud are usually present. The size and type of the particles change a lot from place to place, as they are sifted and graded by the sea.

The features of sand

The first familiar characteristic of damp sand is the useful way it can be moulded into sandcastles with almost vertical walls. Water is so tightly held between the closely packed grains that it does not all flow away but remains as if in a sponge. Sandcastles can have vertical walls because the grains are held together by the same surface tension that causes all small, damp objects to stick to each other. This feature of sand makes it highly suitable for burrowing forms of life. The water held there prevents them drying out at low tide, and the stiffness of damp sand prevents burrows from collapsing.

Sand suitable for building sandcastles is found near the top of the shore where both water and air are held between the grains. Further down the shore the water drains away less freely and no air may be present; so the grains do not stick together and this sand behaves quite differently. (Two damp matchsticks cling together, but not when dipped in a glass of water.) When you stand with bare feet and wiggle your toes on this sort of sand two remarkable things can happen. Either a paler, and apparently drier, region magically appears around your toes, or what was firm sand suddenly turns into a liquid soup.

What has happened is that as nearly half the volume of completely wet sand is composed of water, when you disturb with your toes the way the grains are packed together you may have increased the space between them, which then filled with air. Alternatively, you may have reduced the space between the grains, just like shaking down a jarful of sugar cubes to make room for more. This displaces a lot of water which has nowhere to go, the grains no longer rest against each other, and the area flows like a liquid. This is one reason for the great age of most sand grains. When huge breakers crash onto the beach the grains scarcely touch one another, so they are not worn away nearly as fast as pebbles.

The burrowers

Imagine how useful this property is to burrowing animals. They are protected within a firm, relatively unyielding medium, yet all they have to do is create a small disturbance in the direction they wish to travel, turn the region into a fluid and drag themselves into it. All sorts of different animal groups have devel-oped ways of doing this. So the dreaded 'creepy-crawlies' are by no means absent from sandy beaches: beneath the surface the sand is often teeming with fascinating life forms. It is only beaches exposed to the full fury of the Atlantic Ocean which are so churned by waves that they are almost uninhabited.

Feeding

The way a sandy-shore creature feeds largely determines its way of life. Many filter their food from the sea at high tide, tapping the boundless supply of plankton and decaying fragments of dead animals and plants. The various bivalves (double-shelled relatives of the snails) live like this. They remain buried at a safe depth and extend two tubular siphons to the surface. Water is drawn down one siphon and blown out through the other. Several species use one siphon as a vacuum cleaner to suck up the thin layer of microscopic plants and dead fragments from the surface of the sand. This surface layer is especially noticeable in muddy areas, where all sorts of animals feed on it.

Various types of worm live by swallowing great quantities of sand and digesting from it particles of organic matter. They also digest the huge populations of tiny microscopic creatures that creep and swim in the universe between the sand grains.

The little hunters and scavengers lead busier lives, searching in the sand and on its surface for living prey and dead carrion. Even they are constantly threatened with danger, for at high tide shore crabs and fish such as flat-fish and bass move in on the prowl. At low tide hungry seabirds take their place.

Mud

Particularly large numbers of feeding seabirds are seen on certain shores. Often these shores are sheltered, muddy and gently sloping with a considerable distance between high and low water levels. Birds favour such shores because they support far more animal life than clean, sandy beaches. These huge populations of little animals are related to the presence of the mud and the greenish-brown scum of microscopic plants on its surface. Generally speaking, the muddier a shore, the more life it supports.

The amount of mud mixed with the sand depends on how sheltered a shore is, because waves tend to wash mud away. There is a gradual range from exposed, steeply sloping, sparsely populated beaches of clean sand, to sheltered, flat, densely populated expanses of sticky mud. Pure mud is the most densely populated, but the greatest variety of species is found in slightly muddy sand.

Very muddy areas make different demands on their inhabitants and many sandy-shore animals are not found there. The main difference is the lack of water circulation between the fine particles and the consequent shortage of essential oxygen. To live in mud it is necessary to produce a well-ventilated burrow or extend siphons to the surface. Several inches below the surface of the mud there is no oxygen at all and the bacteria which live there have formed an evil-smelling black layer. Mudflats often form in the shelter of estuaries and the dilution of the seawater prevents many other species from living there.

Only relatively few species live in estuary mudflats, but those that are able to survive here thrive in immense numbers. Such expanses of estuary mud are capable of producing living matter at a greater rate, area for area, than any other environment on earth, and they can have a wild beauty all of their own.

The abundance of bird life is an obvious result of the great productivity of mudflats. The brownish birds with long legs and bills, collectively known as 'waders', are everywhere. The various waders are not the easiest birds to identify. The redshank is common and has conspicuous red legs. The huge flocks of tiny birds that wheel and swerve in the distance like a single organism are often dunlin. The high, sad cries of waders contribute a lot to the desolate atmosphere of this open country, and wildest of all is the cry of the curlew, a bird distinguished by its long, curved bill. Oyster catchers are easier to spot, with their black and white plumage and bright orange bills. Shells of mussels killed by oyster catchers are common on the strand-line. They always have a hole punched in the same position on the edge by that pickaxe of a beak.

During the daytime, the many

174

species of ducks are most often seen floating in groups far away on the water, and the large, dark coloured cormorant and the shy heron are quite unmistakable.

Cockles normally live just under the surface of the sand with two short tubes, or siphons, reaching to the surface. When the tide is in, water is drawn down one tube and expelled through the other. Cockles filter their food from the water in the same way as the **mussel**. The siphons can be seen if you put a few cockles in a bucket of sand and sea water and allow them to bury themselves with their single muscular foot.

It is possible to work out the age of a cockle by counting the rings that run across the rounded, whitish, double shell (not to be confused with the numerous vertical grooves). One ring appears each winter.

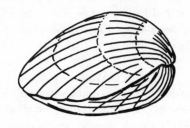

Cockle (*Cerastoderma edule*)

Razorshells are common objects on the strandline of sandy beaches, especially after a storm. They are long, narrow double shells with a papery, brown outer layer which peels off as they dry. The hinge holding the two halves together is near one end, but it becomes very brittle as it dries and the shells are often found singly.

When alive, they live at and below the low-tide mark and are expert burrowers in the sand. A single fleshy foot pushes down into the sand from the lower end, swells, and pulls the animal down an inch or two. In this way it can move downwards very fast and you have to dig like mad to catch

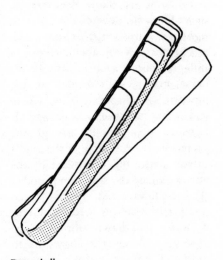

Razorshell

one. Fountains of water betray their presence as you walk past.

Thin tellins are characteristic of the clean mud-free sand of the typical bathing beach. Their tiny, fragile, double shells with bands of pink, orange and white, are a common sight, only 1-2cm, the pairs still joined together and gaping open like butterflies' wings. When alive, they burrow just beneath the surface and may often be there in great numbers, many hundreds beneath a single square foot of sand. Two flexible siphons extend to the surface of the sand, one longer then the other. Water is drawn into the longer siphon, which can either operate like a vacuum cleaner over the surface of the sand, or simply draw in water and plankton.

Thin tellin (*Tellina tenuis*)

Lugworms, growing to over 12cm, are especially common in sheltered areas where the sand is slightly muddy. Large expanses may be covered with their casts — squiggly coils of sand in little heaps. These mark the tail end of the lugworm's U-shaped burrow, where sand that has been swallowed is deposited after passing through the worm's body. A dimple in the sand's surface marks the other end of the burrow, where the lugworm periodically swallows sand, from which food particles are digested. A current of water is drawn through the burrow, enabling the lugworm to breathe. The front part of a lugworm has red, tufted gills and short bristles; the rear is pale and thinner.

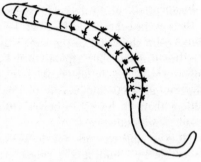

Lugworm (*Arenicola marina*)

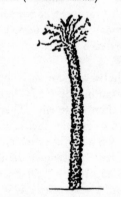

Sandmason worm (*Lanice conchilega*)

Sandmason worms are smaller relatives of the lugworm and ragworm which build themselves durable tubes projecting several inches above the surface of the sand. Some areas are covered with them. The tubes are embedded deep in the sand and have to be dug out carefully to find the worm inside.

At high tide or in an aquarium, long, very thin tentacles extend from the top of the tube in search of food. These same tentacles build the tube out of shell fragments, gravel and sand cemented together with a substance produced from the worm's mouth. The top of each tube has a frayed appearance.

176

Shrimps are sufficiently abundant to be netted in commercial quantities in many areas. Like **prawns**, the pinkish colour only appears after cooking and they are normally sandy coloured and well camouflaged. They spend much of their time buried in the sand with only their eyes and feelers showing. Unlike **prawns** they do not have a jagged spike between the eyes.

Inexpensive shrimp nets (the kind with a wooden crosspiece) can be bought at seaside shops. They are not as efficient as a full-sized shrimp net but work well enough if you hold them almost horizontally against the sand and push forwards as fast as possible through areas of shallow water where shrimps are visible. Small flatfish and common gobies may also be caught.

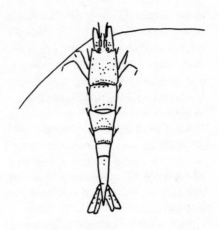

Shrimp (*Crangon vulgaris*)

Common gobies must be familiar to most observant holidaymakers, because they are one of the few species which inhabit shallow, sandy pools on the average bathing beach. The small (about 5cm), sandy-coloured little fish scattering before your feet in such pools are almost certainly common gobies, although, surprisingly, they can easily be confused with the shrimp which is a similar size and colour.

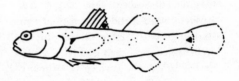

Common goby (*Pomatoschistus minutus*)

These fish also often live in estuaries. Their eggs are laid under an upturned shell and are carefully guarded by the male.

Flatfish are most likely to be seen when you walk quietly beside sandy pools, gullies or the edge of the sea on a calm sunny day. Sooner or later,

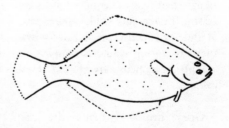

Flatfish

177

there will be a silent underwater explosion of sand and an indefinable shadow will streak out of sight. Until they move, flatfish can be virtually invisible, as they are leaf shaped, with the upper side camouflaged and the underside white.

Small individuals, of postage-stamp size, are most common, as several species of young flatfish spend their first couple of summers in the safe, rich feeding grounds of sheltered bays and estuaries.

Each one is actually lying on its side, and if you look closely at the mouth it can be seen to open sideways.

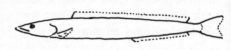

Sand-eel

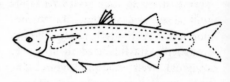

Grey mullet

Sand-eels swim in shoals wherever there is plenty of fine gravel or clean sand. They form an important part of the diet of seabirds and larger fish. Anglers, who spend a lot of their time staring into the edge of the sea, are accustomed to seeing little silvery flashes below the surface as a shoal of sand-eels swims past. Their separate tail fins distinguish them from true eels which have one continuous fin.

The remarkable feature of sand-eels is their ability to burrow into the sand with lightning speed, in order to escape their many enemies. This is the reason for the shovel-like lower jaw. Skilful bait collectors know where they can dig up sand-eels at low tide. Young specimens are found close inshore.

Grey mullet provide the best opportunity for watching really big fish, since they come very close inshore in the summer. On a still day, watch the calm surface of shallow water at the edge of an estuary, harbour or sheltered bay. Monstrous swirls and V-shaped wakes betray the presence of a shoal of streamlined, striped grey mullet. This is a very common sight if you keep your eyes open.

They feed mainly on the microscopic plant life forming the greenish-brown slime on the surface of the mudflats.

178

The **lesser weever** has poisonous spines, whose venom is said to be at least as powerful as that of an adder. If this is so, then the weever qualifies as Britain's most dangerous animal.

It is a small fish, usually less than 10cm long, likely to be encountered in any sandy area where it can find the shrimps it feeds on. The weever buries itself in the sand and an unwary person standing on it with bare feet will be stung by the spines in its front dorsal fin. Anybody handling the fish in a net is also likely to be stung by spines in the fish's gill covers. The symptoms are immediate — intense pain and swelling — but there is no serious danger to life. A recommended treatment is to soak the wound in very hot water to destroy the poison. Anyone who has been stung once is unlikely to let it happen again, but if it does the effects are even more severe the second time.

Use footwear when shrimping and learn to recognise the large, upturned mouth, the deep, narrow body and that wicked black dorsal fin. Do not confuse the weever with the spiny **sea scorpion** of rocky shores, which is harmless, though often persecuted. The **common goby** may be mistaken at first, but it has a smaller mouth and a thinner body than the weever. The larger, offshore, greater weever reaches 45cm in length.

Waders are a large group of birds with long legs and beaks, which are particularly characteristic of the seashore. Their cries are as evocative as the sound of the waves and it is

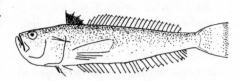

Lesser weever (*Echiichthys vipera*)

Wader

seldom that you can fail to see a group of them feeding at the water's edge or flying in a tight little flock near the horizon. They are present in greatest numbers on muddy shores where food is plentiful, and the inexperienced observer needs binoculars and a good bird book to tell them apart.

The shape of the beak varies, depending on how they feed. For example, the oystercatcher has a stout pickaxe, the curlew has a long probe and the dunlin has delicate tweezers.

Gulls may be seen on all types of shore, eating small living creatures, dead animals and refuse. Several kinds of gull are now more common than ever — all with long, slender wings and pale plumage. They have greatly benefited from their habit of eating refuse, and whole populations are almost totally dependent on today's big rubbish dumps.

On the shore, they eat a wide variety of animals. Look out for gulls repeatedly flying up and dropping mussels or cockles to break their shells. Shore crabs are another favourite food.

Gull

Young gulls have brown, speckled plumage which does not whiten until their third or fourth year.

Hermit crab, with its soft abdomen inside an empty whelk shell for protection

Strandline after a storm which has washed up many starfish and mussels (*Rodger Jackman/Wildlife Picture Agency*)

Flounder, one of several flatfish common in sandy and muddy habitats

Sand dunes stabilised by marram grass provide excellent nesting sites for certain sea birds (*Leslie Jackman/Wildlife Picture Agency*)

Xanthoria, a lichen, occurs on the splash zone rocks and above in coarse, orange encrustations

Ramelina, another lichen, forms greenish-grey, stiff tufts which, on sheltered rocks, can reach several inches. It grows slightly higher up than *Xanthoria*, though the two often overlap, as here

Collecting wildlife in a rocky pool

Rhizostoma pulmo, the largest British jellyfish which can reach 60cm across but is completely harmless. It is common on south and west coasts

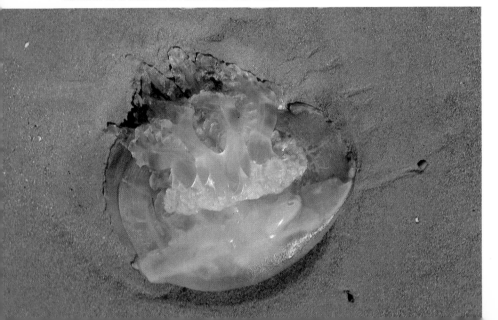

Seaweeds

Seaweeds are probably the most conspicuous and familiar forms of life on rocky shores, particularly where there is shelter from big waves. On sandy and muddy shores, they grow only on solid objects like isolated boulders or wooden posts.

The holdfast

Seaweeds never root themselves in sand or mud, only occasionally appearing to do so when attached to a buried stone. This is a fundamental difference from land plants, which are rooted in soil and draw essential chemicals from it. Seaweeds extract the chemicals they need directly from the seawater around them. Rather than a system of roots, they have what is known as a holdfast, which fastens them to the rock very securely. The holdfast may be disc-shaped or may sometimes resemble a tangled mass of roots, as with the oarweed. However, its function is purely to fasten down the plant, not to absorb water and nutrients.

Zonation

All seaweeds are water plants which would die if they were not regularly submerged by the rise and fall of the tide. Obviously, the higher up the shore a seaweed lives, the more time it spends out of water and the greater its exposure to drying out, wave action, temperature extremes, rainwater and all the other hazards of the seashore. This is why each species is adapted to survive at a particular level on the shore.

Such zonation of the commonest seaweeds is obvious at low tide on any rocky shore. Going from high-tide level to low-tide level usually involves walking through distinctive zones of each of the following common species: channelled wrack, flat wrack (upper shore), bladder wrack and/or knotted wrack (middle shore), and finally saw wrack, oarweeds and red seaweeds (lower shore).

Lichens are not actually seaweeds but a strange example of cooperation between different life forms; a dry, encrusting rock growth — part-fungus and part-plant. They cannot tolerate polluted air near cities but are common everywhere in the countryside. Several species are particularly characteristic of the upper shore,

185

where they bring bright patches of colour to the rocks.

A few types often form distinct bands at different levels. The black colour of rocks on the top half of the shore is usually due to an extensive covering of *Verrucaria*. *Xanthoria* often forms a bright orange band just above high-tide level. Slightly higher up, there may be stringy little tufts of pale green *Ramalina*.

Channelled wrack lives so far up the shore that it is only submerged by spring tides. It grows in small tufts, with a distinct channel along the underside of each little frond. In some exposed areas it lives where even the highest spring tides do not reach it, and relies on being regularly doused with spray. After a long spell of calm, sunny weather, especially during neap tides, channelled wrack can become dark, dry and brittle. As soon as it is wetted again, it absorbs water quickly and regains its normal appearance.

Flat wrack is almost always to be found in a narrow zone just below the band of **channelled wrack**, on the upper shore. It has flat, twisted fronds, with smooth edges and no air bladders.

Like all the other types of wrack, swollen, pale areas are often to be seen at the tips of the fronds. These contain countless tiny eggs and sperms which are released into the water when ripe. The fertilised eggs become microscopic young plants which swim with the plankton for a while before settling down.

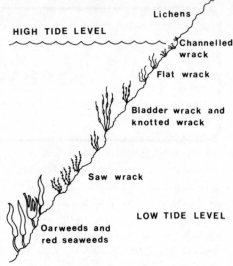

Zonation of seaweeds

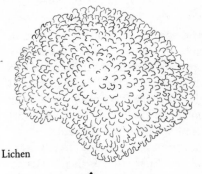

Lichen

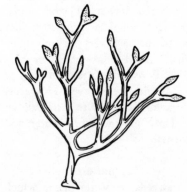

Channelled wrack (*Pelvetia canaliculata*)

186

It only seems strange to think of tiny, actively swimming young plants because this habit was abandoned by the more familiar plants which have invaded dry land.

Bladder wrack, found on the middle shore, is lifted up towards the light at high tide by the little bladders which give it extra buoyancy and distinguish it from flat wrack. Flat winkles are often seen among the bladders. It is possible to work out roughly how old a plant is by counting the number of times a frond has branched between its tip and the holdfast. Fronds of bladder wrack usually branch twice each year.

The lower parts of old plants are often worn away, leaving only the tough middle rib of each frond.

Knotted wrack, with its large air bladders, may be found together with bladder wrack on the middle shore. It is particularly abundant in sheltered areas where it can grow as long as five feet and cover the rocks with a tangled blanket. Its fronds have no middle rib and its fruiting parts are on short stalks along the fronds. At high tide it floats up to form a dense jungle. Tufts of a fine, dark red seaweed are often seen growing on this species.

The typical heavy growths of knotted wrack take a long time to become established and do not immediately return when an oil slick is cleared away.

Flat wrack (*Fucus spiralis*)

Bladder wrack (*Fucus vesiculosus*)

Knotted wrack (*Ascophyllum nodosum*)

187

Saw wrack has flattened fronds with jagged edges, and no air bladders. It grows at the lower end of the shore and is an excellent indication that you are in a good zone to look for seashore animals. (If **bladder wrack** or **knotted wrack** are at the water's edge then the best hunting grounds are under water.)

Thousands of very small, white, spiral tubes are often attached to the fronds of saw wrack. Little worms called *Spirorbis* live inside these tubes and will extend their fan-like tentacles if placed in seawater.

Saw wrack (*Fucus serratus*)

Oarweeds grow on the lower shore and become visible only during spring tides. They are immediately obvious because they are big plants with thick stems and flat leathery blades in various shapes. They look positively uncomfortable out of water, lying in loops like an endless tangled hosepipe. Strong stems and powerful holdfasts prevent the oarweeds from being washed away by even the biggest waves.

The rootlike holdfasts provide shelter and hiding places for all sorts of small creatures. This region of the shore continues to hold surprises long after the commoner seashore animals have become relatively familiar.

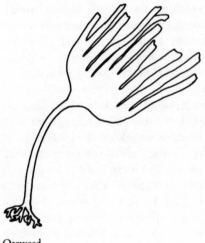

Oarweed

Red seaweeds grow on the lower shore, on and among **oarweeds,** and they show how rewarding it is to look at everything really closely when exploring the shore. If it is a spring tide and you are able to reach the red-seaweed zone, it is well worth examining the tremendous variety of these beautiful plants. There are hundreds of species.

It is easy to make beautiful displays of pressed red seaweeds on paper or white cardboard. Simply arrange the specimens on the card, cover with a sheet or two of newspaper and leave under a pile of books for a few days.

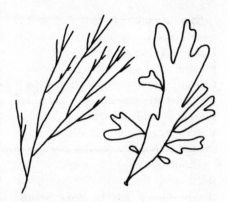

Red seaweeds

Enteromorpha has bright green tubular fronds and is one of the commonest of the green seaweeds, especially where the water is brackish — in high pools or streams. **Sea lettuce** is another green seaweed which grows in thin, crumpled, flat sheets. In summer they grow much faster than the various brown seaweeds and can cover large areas.

Where limpets are present in any numbers, *Enteromorpha* grows in the only place safe from their browsing — on the shells of the limpets themselves. When no limpets are present, for example if they have been killed off by oil or detergent, whole areas of the shore quickly turn green.

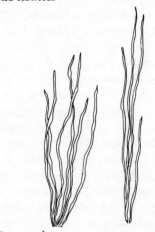

Enteromorpha

Strandline

Beachcombing can be done at any time, regardless of the state of the tide. You can take it slowly on a warm day, searching on your hands and knees for tiny shells, or you can stride along in the teeth of a gale to see what the storm has brought in. When the waves are big, the undertow becomes strong enough to affect the normally tranquil seabed below the low-tide level. The remains of all sorts of less familiar creatures, not normally seen on the shore, are washed up. Looking at these clues, it is possible to form an impression of the mysterious grounds beyond the shore.

Often, the strandline is marked by dark lines of drying seaweed, rolled into rough sausage-shapes by the waves. Entangled with the seaweed there may be other growths, similar but much paler. These are animal growths such as hydroids and horn-wrack. Other finds are scattered among the lines of weed.

Shells
Shell collecting can be a rewarding hobby, with the aim of finding as many species as possible. Some beaches are more productive than others — places where rocky and sandy areas meet are usually the best, as each produces characteristic shells. On the first day you may find a dozen species, then things will slow down. With some diligence and visits to different areas you should be able to find forty or fifty types, and there are still far, far more to be found. Framed, labelled collections can be very attractive. Any inhabited shells found can be cleared after being boiled. For identification, consult *Collins Pocket Guide to the Sea Shore.*

Only after many serious visits to the shore are you likely to make such unusual finds as Britain's largest shell, the fan mussel, twelve inches long and fan shaped. Another rarity is the violet sea snail, which floats on the surface of the open Atlantic and whose fragile shell seldom survives the surf.

Junk
Plenty of man's debris comes ashore, unsightly but often interesting. It is a guessing game for all ages to play, trying to deduce the origin of all sorts of mysterious water-worn objects.

190

Any strandline shows that this is very much the age of plastic, which survives in the sea for years on end. Some junk has simply been carried along from somewhere further down the coast. Other stuff has been thrown overboard by ships at sea or may be the remains of a shipwreck. Strange, large beans are found from time to time, which are believed to originate from the West Indies and South America. Last summer I found an American car tyre covered with long, stalked, goose barnacles which grow on objects drifting in the open Atlantic.

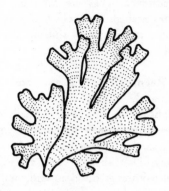

Hornwrack (*Flustra foliacea*)

Oil
As a result of man's carelessness, sticky lumps of congealed oil are now floating about in all the oceans of the world and can be found on any strandline. Local spillages or discharges are more disastrous, and numbers of dead and dying seabirds may be washed up. When the oil slick itself comes ashore, the clearing-up operations are geared towards cleaning the sandy beaches for holidaymakers, and the detergent which is so liberally applied poisons the creatures which have avoided being smothered by the oil. Oil and detergent pose the greatest single threat to our seashore wildlife.

Hornwrack is easily mistaken for a plant as it resembles bunches of dry, sandy-coloured seaweed. It is present on most strandlines, mixed with seaweed, but it can be recognised by its pale colour. Looking very closely,

you can see the thousands of tiny chambers into which it is divided. Each chamber is occupied by a little animal which feeds on minute drifting plankton. Each frond of hornwrack is therefore an animal colony.

Many of the animals which feed on plankton look plantlike because there is no need for them to move around.

Hydroids are another example of plantlike animal colonies which feed on plankton. There are many kinds and most are branched, although one species resembles a lobster's feelers. Their thin, often feathery shape distinguishes them from the flattened **hornwrack**. All hydroids have a jointed appearance: each joint is occupied by an animal resembling a tiny sea anemone, complete with little tentacles for feeding.

Like the great majority of animals in the sea, hydroids have a young stage when they drift with other plankton before settling on a suitable surface and taking on the adult

191

appearance. They are commonest on rocky seabeds, but will also grow on stones and shells in shifting sand or mud.

Mermaids' purses are the flattened, oblong egg cases of the dogfish, skate and ray. Normally only the empty case is found, the young fish having hatched out and swum away. Dogfish egg cases are a pale yellowish-brown, elongated, with a long tangled thread at each corner. The threads anchor the egg case among growths like seaweed and hydroids on the seabed. The much darker mermaid's purses with only four short horns at the corners belong to the skates and rays, usually the thornback ray.

Sponges also do not need to move around because they live by filtering plankton from the water. Irregularly shaped, they go hard and brown when dry. They are organised like a colony of microscopic animal cells, supported on a framework of tiny slivers of lime or glass, depending on the species. (The familiar bath sponge is a warm-water species with a more flexible horny skeleton which does not go so hard when it dries out.)

To feed, water is driven through the maze of internal passages and blown out through the larger holes on the outside.

Common whelk eggs are a familiar sight, especially during spring. They are straw-coloured, pea-sized capsules laid on the seabed in

Hydroids

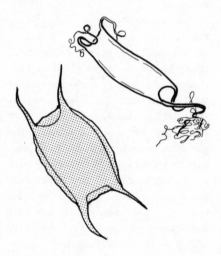

Mermaids' purses

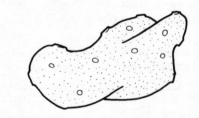

Sponge

192

masses about the size of a tennis ball, which are very light when dry. Larger masses are often produced by several whelks together.

Each little capsule in the mass contains about a thousand eggs, but only about ten perfectly formed little snails eventually emerge from each capsule, having fed on the other eggs. It is usually only the empty capsules that are seen on the strandline.

Common whelk eggs (*Buccinum undatum*)

Common whelk shells are large, brown or white snail shells with prominent ridges on each coil. They are abundant in most sandy areas. Unlike the **dog whelk**, they usually live below the low-tide level, where they prey on other molluscs and generally scavenge for food. Commercial fishermen trap them in baited pots. The larger hermit crabs often occupy their empty shells.

The shells become partially broken by the pounding they have received, and the graceful internal structure of a typical snail shell is revealed. Like nearly all shells, the shape is mathematically perfect, exactly following a formula by which the width at any point is proportional to the turns made by the spiral.

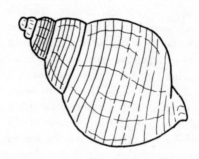

Common whelk shell

Large tunnels several centimetres in diameter may be seen in softer rocks such as limestone. Sometimes the paired, white shells of the piddock, a mollusc, may still be visible inside. A tiny boring **sponge** makes pinhead sized holes in limestone and empty shells. Oyster shells are often riddled by it.

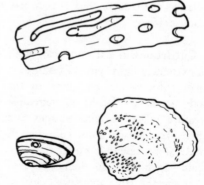

Shells, stones and pieces of wood with holes in them

Small holes in driftwood are probably made by the gribble, a relative of the familiar woodlouse causing great damage to boats and piers. Larger holes in driftwood from the open sea are made by the shipworm, another mollusc.

Single, circular holes in the occasional empty little shell are often evidence of an attack by the predatory snail known as the necklace shell.

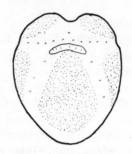

Sea potato (*Echinocardium cordatum*)

Sea potatoes are a kind of sea urchin — relatives of the **starfish** which have lost their five arms. The little bony plates which cover the body of a starfish have become fused together to form the sea potato's shell. Their bodies, about 5cm wide, are covered with movable little spines and tube feet similar to those of the starfish, but there is normally hardly any sign of these on their delicate, white heart-shaped shells which are patterned with furrows and rows of little holes.

Sea potatoes live in shallow burrows at the lower end of mud-free sandy beaches.

Cuttlebone is flat and oval, with an extremely light, porous texture. It gives stiffness and buoyancy to the body of the cuttlefish, an incredible creature related to the octopus and squid. Cuttlefish, quite common in sandy areas, resemble rather flattened squid with similar sucker-covered arms and the same amazing ability to change colour in a split second. They have big, intelligent eyes and are merciless hunters of animals like

Cuttlebone (*Sepia officinalis*)

shrimps, small fish and crabs.

The animal controls its buoyancy by regulating the relative amounts of water and gas in the spaces inside the cuttlebone.

Jellyfish are transparent discs of jelly with brown or bluish markings, the largest planktonic animals, with little control over where the sea carries them. Their bodies are nearly all water and in hot weather they are soon reduced to nothing more than circular marks in the sand. Watch an undamaged one in the water to appreciate the full beauty of the pulsating bell and undulating tentacles. The mouth is underneath, surrounded by four long frills.

The species which sting have long trailing tentacles, but the commonest species has short tentacles and four bluish circles in the bell. It feeds on small plankton and does not sting.

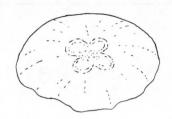

Sandhoppers are small shrimp-like creatures which hop madly when rotting seaweed is disturbed. They are true residents of the strandline and prefer to advance still further up the shore during extra high tides, to avoid the waves. Very similar species live under stones lower down the shore, but these are not such powerful jumpers and are covered at high tide.

Jellyfish

The true sandhoppers of the strandline have presumably developed the ability to jump in order to escape the turnstones and plovers which hunt for them. To do this, the spiked tail is curved forward and set against the sand. Then the body springs straight, catapulting the animal several feet. The effect of swarms of sandhoppers doing this must be very confusing to any bird trying to catch them.

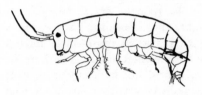

Sandhopper (*Talitrus saltator*)

The **sea slater** and the **bristletail** hide away in crevices above high-tide level and come out mostly at night. The sea slater is a crustacean, closely related to the woodlouse. The bristletail, which has three long hairs on its tail, is an insect, related to the silverfish seen around the hearths of old houses.

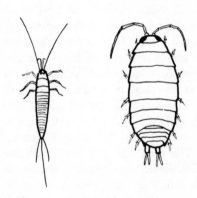

Bristletail (*Petrobius maritimus*) (*left*) and sea slater (*Ligia oceanica*)

Other animals live, like the **sand-hopper**, under piles of rotting seaweed. Brownish centipedes may be seen and flies and beetles breed there.

195

Investigating seashore life

Investigation of the seashore should not be thought of as the exclusive right of professional marine biologists. In fact, a considerable amount of our present knowledge of shore life was contributed by Victorian amateur naturalists. Scientists nowadays tend to ignore amateur investigations, largely because they require professional standards of accuracy and detail. Also, there is now so much scientific literature about marine life that it is very difficult for an amateur to find out if any of his discoveries have been described before. Never mind – there is so much pleasure in finding out for oneself about the mysterious lives of the vast range of sea creatures that this scarcely matters.

The first thing is to familiarise oneself with as many species as possible, in a wide range of environments. Here, the sole use of this book has its limitations. The commonest species are described here: so also are representatives of most major groups, so that an unfamiliar specimen may at least be recognised as 'an anemone', for example, or 'a bivalve mollusc'. The excellent *Collins Pocket Guide to the Sea Shore* has

already been recommended for identification of many more species.

When you get used to a particular shore it is possible to become quite cocky about your ability to identify everything in sight – animals and plants. Beware when you reach this stage, because it is only an illusion, as certain species are present in far greater profusion than others. Just search a little more carefully, cover more ground and spend more time. Unfamiliar specimens will appear again and again in a very humbling manner, especially on a sheltered rocky shore. A single lifetime is not long enough to learn them all, and herein lies the fascination of the subject.

Efforts should be made to understand more about the *lives* of the shore's inhabitants as well as their names, or we will be little better than train-spotters or stamp-collectors. Knowledge of the name of a specimen is of little value on its own. The aquarium has always been the biggest help here, next to keen observation and careful recording. For our purposes there are three types: the field aquarium, used for observation on the shore; the temporary aquarium, for keeping specimens alive for several days; and the permanent aquarium.

The field aquarium
The best field aquarium, as any youngster will inform you, is the jam jar. It is a delicate piece of equipment which must be handled with care on a slippery shore, so a clear plastic sandwich box may be used by the less traditionally minded. The creatures you see on the shore are waiting for the returning sea to cover them. The animals are generally huddled and inactive and the smaller plants (and plantlike animal growths) are hanging as shapeless blobs on rock surfaces. Even those specimens in pools are hard to see through the rippling surface, and are often camouflaged.

Transfer your find to the field aquarium and see the difference. A captured prawn which had haunted the corner of a pool like a drab ghost is revealed as a graceful and intricate form, its transparent body jewelled with colours. 'Like a little fairy', I once heard an awestruck seaside landlady exclaim. It is worth examining the workings of the prawn's many different limbs. Some are used for swimming and egg-carrying, others for walking, feeding and defence, while yet others have evolved into highly complicated mouthparts. To move, the prawn crawls and glides and occasionally flicks backwards. The algae it has eaten is usually visible as a green patch in the stomach. All this and much

more comes to light as soon as the prawn is placed in the jam jar.

If a small stone or shell encrusted with barnacles is viewed underwater in the jar, it is not long before the barnacles begin to feed. Each little 'trapdoor' opens and a bunch of feathery cirri repeatedly rake the water for plankton. These cirri have evolved from the legs of the barnacles' shrimp-like ancestor. The feeding tentacles of *Spirorbis* worms can also be seen, if a piece of saw wrack bearing the tiny, white, coiled tubes is immersed in the jar.

Most snails and limpets become active at once when placed in water. Then, against the glass, can be seen the mysterious waves of contraction that cause the muscular foot to glide along and, better still, the feeding movements of the mouth and the rasping tongue. I have noticed that most snails immediately crawl upwards when dropped in a jar of water – this is just one example of a simple observation that could stimulate all sorts of conjectures and further experiments. The most sluggish snail can usually be stimulated into activity by touching it with a small starfish. (It is impossible to see how a starfish moves without watching its system of tube feet through glass.)

Anemones can usually be removed from a rock by careful use of a thumbnail. Provided the base is undamaged, they will open out quite soon and can be fed with pieces of crushed winkle or limpet. The food 'sticks' to the tentacles because of

197

their countless microscopic stinging cells which shoot out tiny threads on contact.

Many shapeless, soggy blobs hanging from rock surfaces are actually finely branching growths, whose beauty is only revealed underwater. They may be red, green or brown seaweeds. Other growths have the sandy colour typical of many microscopic animal colonies — hydroids or feathery bryozoans (related to the familiar hornwrack of the strandline).

A couple of inches of sand at the bottom of a jar of water make it possible to see the burrowing skills of some of the inhabitants of sand. Keep the jar still, and with patience you can watch a cockle dig itself in with its fleshy, inflatable foot. After a while, only the tips of two siphon tubes remain visible at the surface for feeding. Even they are retracted at the slightest disturbance.

Shrimps disappear under the sand much more quickly. Swimming straight to the bottom of the jar, they make a scrabbling motion with their limbs and sink rapidly out of sight until only their feelers and eyestalks remain visible above the surface. Small flatfish do much the same — one quick wriggle, and a puff of sand swirls up to settle on top of them.

If a small weever is ever captured, its hiding behaviour can also be studied in the jar — but under no circumstances must it be directly handled, because of its highly venomous spines. Using the fins beneath its body, it makes sideways snuggling movements and sinks down quickly like the shrimp.

The temporary aquarium

It is possible to keep the smallest creatures alive for several days in a jam jar, but in general it is only useful for observing specimens before setting them free again. A larger container is necessary to keep animals alive for any longer.

The usual problem in an overcrowded jar is shortage of oxygen. If the supply of this vital gas dissolved in the water is used up faster than it can be replenished from the air, the occupants of the jar will suffocate. So, avoid putting too many specimens in a small volume of water: even a single shrimp is 'overcrowded' in a jam jar if it is to remain there for any length of time. Larger containers such as sweet jars and washing-up bowls are more suitable for a temporary home aquarium. Of these, the bowls are a better shape because of the greater area of water surface through which oxygen can be replenished from the air.

The temperature must be watched, partly because oxygen is less soluble in warm seawater. Seashore animals are more tolerant of high temperatures than their offshore cousins, but care is still needed.

In spite of all this, your specimens will still probably die in a few days, as the water is gradually poisoned by the dissolved excretory products of the animals and the chemicals formed by the decomposition of dead organic matter. The Victorian naturalists

198

solved this by observing scrupulous hygiene, clearing all dead matter from the aquarium and allowing large volumes of water for each specimen. Bacteria and other micro-organisms in the community were then able to maintain the water's balanced state by breaking down the toxic waste chemicals into harmless ones. Regular, routine seawater changes were also carried out. All this needed dedication, but the Victorian amateur aquarium craze produced some very successful results.

It is not necessary to go to all this trouble for a temporary aquarium in which specimens will only be kept for a day or so before being returned to the shore. All sorts of containers may be used, provided they are large enough and not made of metal (most metals are poisonous to sea creatures). Pure seawater must be used. Any mud will quickly settle out, but the water must not be taken from an area likely to be diluted with fresh water.

It is easy to learn more about the lives of seashore animals when there is time to study them in the comfort of your home. Many have internal clocks adjusting their behaviour to the rhythm of the tides. Do your captive anemones open and other creatures become active at the time of high tide? For more obvious results, you can make the tide ebb and flow in your temporary aquarium.

No member of a seashore community ought to be studied on its own. It is important to see how it interacts with its neighbours, of the same and other species. Everybody talks a lot about the law of the jungle, implying endless, cut-throat competition, but co-operation and interdependence between species are also apparent in any jungle. The same applies on the seashore.

The hermit crab carries around the empty shell of a dead snail for protection. The shell is often inhabited by at least three other animal species which share the crab's food: a ragworm which helps to keep the shell clean inside, an anemone which gives some camouflage and stinging protection, and a furry hydroid colony encrusting the outside of the shell. The crab, snail, ragworm, anemone and hydroid depend on one another in this close relationship. Many quite different animals can be surprisingly tolerant of one another. They have to be when they are crowded together under a rock at low tide. Introduce some large blennies or other rockpool fish into a container stocked with beadlet anemones. The fish brush against the tentacles without any sign of being stung. Try the same experiment with young flatfish from a sandy shore which do not normally encounter beadlet anemones. You can see the tentacles sticking to their skin, even though larger fish usually break free.

Beadlet anemones certainly interact with one another. They space themselves out to ensure plenty of space to feed. Watch them using the blue 'beads' around the base of the tentacles to chase away a neighbour who is too close — deliberate touching with one or two of the blue beads seems to do the trick.

Soft estuary mud might seem an unlikely subject for the temporary aquarium, but it is invariably covered with holes, spoil heaps and mysterious, meandering little tracks. Make a layer a couple of inches deep at the bottom of a plastic bowl of seawater, stir well and allow the thick, brown soup to settle overnight. By morning the water will be surprisingly clear and the first markings will already have arrived on the surface of the mud.

Various worms will have perforated the surface with their burrows, and some may be seen leaving winding trails as they move about in the open. Many of the holes will be entrances to the 5cm-deep, U-shaped burrows of *Corophium*, a little relative of the sandhoppers with huge feelers. Various burrowing bivalves will have taken up their stations, with double siphon tubes extending to the top of the mud. The peppery furrow shell

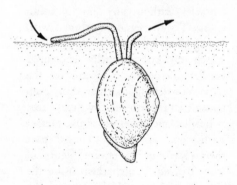

'Vacuum cleaner' feeding by peppery furrow shell *(Scrobicularia plana)*

forms a star-shaped pattern where one of its siphons sweeps up surrounding debris like a vacuum cleaner. Small snails also emerge from the mud to go about their business. This is the important community that feeds those thousands of estuary seabirds and hungry fish.

The permanent aquarium
A permanent display of living seashore creatures *is* within everyone's capability, and it does not need the same continuous attention as the old Victorian version. The home aquarium has been revolutionised by the small electric air pump. Not only will it supply oxygen to the water by bubbling; it may also be used to operate a biological filter (*see* diagram) The 'air lift tube' draws water from under the perforated plastic base beneath the gravel. Water flows down through the gravel, where it is chemically purified by the massive population of microscopic life on the gravel particles. An aquarium like this needs only occasional water changes and is surprisingly easy to maintain. Very little has been written this century about keeping British marine life in home aquaria, which is a great pity. *Sea Water Aquaria* by Leslie Jackman (David & Charles) is worth having, though it is rather dated and does not deal with the vital topic of biological filtration.

The following hints should prevent most serious mistakes.
Use the largest aquarium possible.
Avoid metal-framed tanks.

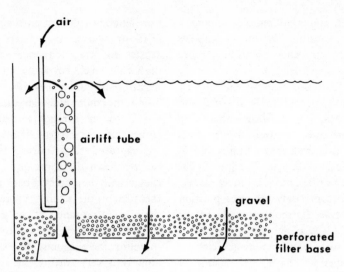

Biological filter

Look for gravel with particles of approximately matchhead size.

Check the salinity of the seawater with a hydrometer (obtained from an aquarium dealer) and maintain it between 1.020 and 1.025, adding tapwater occasionally to counteract evaporation.

Set the aquarium up away from bright light to avoid excessive algal growth, and do not waste time trying to keep seaweed alive.

Deep frozen mussels and limpets are a convenient food.

Never overfeed, and make a pair of wooden forceps to remove uneaten food and dead specimens.

Watch for slightly milky water. This is a sign of low oxygen level, probably caused by something decaying or an overstocked aquarium. High temperatures make matters worse. Attend to the problem at once and increase aeration if possible.

Avoid contamination of the water with poisonous substances such as soap and metals.

Try to change half the water every few weeks.

A typical rocky shore collection in a 2ft, 12-gallon aquarium might be as follows: six beadlet anemones, six prawns, two small hermit crabs, two starfish and two blennies. Alternatively, an estuary community might be set up in a similar tank with a sandy bottom. This could contain six shrimps, six 4cm flounders, six common gobies, four 5cm grey mullet. These are only guides because the possibilities are infinite.

Observations on the shore

Careful observation on the shore is just as important and it is quite easy to watch all sorts of seashore species as they go about their work. The twice-daily rise and fall of the tide imposes a regular routine, so, many animals commute to and from the secure homes they occupy at low tide. Accurate record-keeping and the use of coloured paint to mark snail and limpet shells soon shows this. Top shells are most common under stones at low tide, and they climb round to the upper surfaces to feed on algae when the tide is in. A limpet always returns to precisely the same position at low tide. Its shell grows to fit the shape of the rock exactly and often wears away a characteristic, circular scar. Scientists have been unable to discover any simple explanation for the limpet's unerring ability to find its way home. This would be a good topic for amateur investigation.

It is important for each animal to remain in its particular zone at the correct level of the shore. Winkles often live on sheltered mud flats where there is no noticeable slope to help them maintain their correct position relative to high and low tide levels. When they begin feeding, they have been observed to move first towards the sun and later away from it. In this way, they leave a U-shaped track and finish up close to their original position. Other winkles on vertical surfaces first move downwards and later upwards, achieving the same result. There is some evidence that winkles have surprisingly good eyesight, and may use distant vision to regulate their position on the shore. There is scope for all sorts of experiments here.

There is no doubt about the excellent eyesight of the sandhopper (*Talitrus saltator*). These little crustaceans live in the sand above the high tide level, emerging to feed at night. Although they wander far down the shore when feeding, they return to the strandline before the rising tide covers them. If individuals are captured there during the day, carried down the shore and released, they usually hop quickly back towards the top of the shore, whatever the slope of the sand. It is generally thought that they are able to see the shoreline itself against the sky, but nobody is very sure. Once again, all sorts of experiments suggest themselves.

The inhabitants of sandy or rocky pools can easily be watched and soon ignore your presence if you keep still. A really worthwhile project would be to choose a single rock pool, remote from any likelihood of human interference, and follow the changes in its population through the year. The pool need only be a small one, so that the position of every visible animal and seaweed can be marked on a series of maps, at say, monthly intervals.

Transects
A transect is the traditional way of studying the vertical zonation of life on the shore. It is easiest to obtain clear results on a relatively even surface such as a steep, flat rock face, a harbour wall or a pier stanchion. First stretch out a line marked off at metre intervals. The idea is to find the approximate number of each species

per square metre at various levels. You need a wooden or metal frame enclosing an area of one square metre and another of one square decimetre (a square with 10cm sides).

At measured intervals along the transect line, lay down the square metre frame and identify the animals and plants within it. For seaweeds, it is sufficient to estimate the percentage of the total area in the frame covered by each species. Animals should normally be counted. It may be impractical to count all the numerous small animals like barnacles or young mussels in a square metre, so use the square decimetre frame and multiply the result by 100. Remember that this is a case where sensible estimates are just as valuable as time-wasting attempts to be over-accurate. The results may be set out in vertical columns with the name of a species or group (eg barnacles) at the head of each column, and distances down the transect marked at the side.

An intertidal nature trail
The basic idea of a nature trail is to guide people around a given area, while explaining various items of interest. Seashore nature trails are uncommon, but there is great scope for them. It is not usually possible or desirable to litter the shore with explanatory signs or numbered 'stations', so the best approach is to produce a duplicated or photocopied leaflet in conjunction with a clear, simple map of the shore. These guides could be produced for use by a school or seaside shops might be persuaded to sell them for you. In view of the growing dangers of pollution, anything that increases public interest in marine life is well worth doing.

Choose a shore that is easily accessible, and which has not already

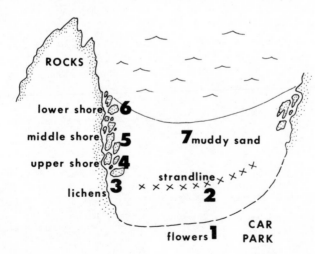

Simple map to accompany a seashore nature trail

been ruined by bait-digging anglers or 'educational' groups failing to replace overturned rocks. A sheltered, rocky habitat should be included and if an area of muddy sand is nearby, so much the better.

Work out a route that can demonstrate all the interesting features in a reasonably logical order, and mark a number on the map at each place you want your visitors to pause. The written guide should begin with a brief summary of the main features of this particular shore, before directing the reader to the starting point. The trail illustrated here takes us from the top of the shore down towards the low tide mark, describing the main plants and animals visible at each level as we go along. Finally, for contrast, it draws attention to the various inhabitants of the thriving muddy sand population at the centre of this sheltered bay.

It is vital that a guide of this sort should explain the importance, when searching, of replacing rocks without overturning them.

INDEX

dunnock, 140

earwig, 44
eel, 96–7; conger, 11; sand, 178
elder, 117, 121–2
elm, 110, 117, 118
Evelyn, John, 117

fern, 34–5, 79, 130, 135
flag iris, 67, 78, 79
flatfish, 174, 177–8, 182, 198
flatworm, 73–4, 81, 85, 100, 105, 108
flounder, 182, 201
fly, 41, 51, 126, 134–5, 153, 195
fox, 6, 8, 56, 59, 114, 144, 146, 148
foxglove, 33, 129
frog, 8, 52, 53, 95
frogbit, 69
froghopper, 43, 44
fulmar, 163
fungus, 34, 136
furze, 111; *see also* gorse

gannet, 163
goby, common, 177, 179, 201
goldfinch, 138
gorse, 122–3
grass, 29, 30, 35
grasshopper, 43–4
grebe, great crested, 95
greenfinch, 138
greenfly, 41, 42
gribble, 194
groundsel, 31, 134
guillemot, 163
gull, 18, 163, 180

harvestman, 25, 50
hawks beard, 130
hawthorn, 109–11, 114, 117, 119–21
hay infusion, 93
hazel, 119–20, 137
hedgehog, 8, 40, 55–6, 59, 114, 144–6, 148, 149
herb robert, 133
herbicides, 33, 116

heron, 175
holly, 111, 120
honeysuckle, 126
hornwort, 68, 69
hornwrack, 190, 191, 198
hossetail, 34–5
hoverfly, 7, 10, 28, 41, 49
hydra, 74, 99
hydroid, 190–2, 198, 199

insecticides, 21, 48–9, 52, 55, 108
ivy, 20, 125–6

jack-by-the-hedge, 136, 151
Jackman, Leslie, 200
jellyfish, 74, 166, 184, 194–5

kestrel, 114, 143
kingfisher, 95

ladybird, 42, 49
leaf miner, 27
leatherjacket, 42
leech, 9, 74, 81, 87, 98, 99, 100
lettuce, sea, 189
lichen, 8, 28, 34, 35, 130, 183, 185–6
limpet, 156, 157, 159, 165, 166, 189, 197, 202; river, 81
lizard, 53, 149, 150
loach, 75, 97
loosestrife, 77
lugworm, 176

magpie, 114, 142, 147
maple, 117, 119, 123
may tree *see* hawthorn
mayfly, 72, 75, 76, 88, 100, 105
mermaids' purse, 192
microscope, 89–91, 104
midge, 86–7, 107
millipede, 37
minnow, 61, 75, 96, 98
mite, 38; water 72–4, 99
mole, 55, 145
moorhen, 94
mosquito, 42, 85, 99, 153

moss, 12, 34–5; water, 75
moth, 46–7, 57–8, 115, 126
mouse, 8, 40, 54–5, 115, 119, 137, 145; field/wood, 147–8; harvest 148–9
mullet, grey, 178, 201
mushroom, 34
mussel, 157, 162, 165, 166, 169, 174, 175, 181, 203; fan, 190; freshwater, 87–8

nettle, 20, 31, 32, 49, 115, 141, 152
newt, 8, 9, 52, 95, 96, 98
nightshade, 7, 128
nipplewort, 7
nuthatch, 120, 139

oak, 20, 117, 137
oarweed, 185, 188
otter, 94
owl, 40, 58–9, 114, 137, 139, 147, 148
oyster catcher, 174, 179

parsley, 131, 132
peppery furrow shell, 200
perch, 97
pesticides, 37
piddock, 193
pigeon, wood, 18, 126, 137
plankton, 66, 159, 162, 166, 173, 191, 192
plantain, lamb's tongue, 130
pollution, 9, 13, 60, 105–8, 191, 203
polypody, 135, 136
pond skater, 80, 83–4
pondweed, 68, 69
porpoise, 163
potato, sea, 184
prawn, 156, 167–9, 177, 197, 201
primrose, 110
privet, 122
puffin, 163

rabbit, 33, 114, 134, 144, 145
ragworm, 169–70, 199
ragwort, 30–1
rat, 40, 54, 115, 145, 146
ray, 192

razorbill, 163
razorshell, 175
redshank, 174
reed, common, 67
reedmace, 67–8
roach, 97
robin, 139–40
rook, 137, 142–3
rose, wild, 124–5
rosebay willowherb, 31
rotifer, 93
roundworm, 87, 93

sandhopper, 73, 167, 195, 202
scorpion, sea, 170, 171, 179; water, 72–3, 99
sea slater, 195
seal, 163
seaweed, 156, 157, 159, 163, 166, 172, 185–91, 198, 203; *see also* under individual headings
shark, 163
'shave' 'shaw', 111
shipworm, 194
shrew, 10, 55, 145, 146–7, 149; water, 94
shrimp, 177, 194, 198, 201; freshwater, 73, 76, 98, 100, 105
skate, 192
sloe *see* blackthorn
slow-worm, 7, 8, 53, 145, 149–50
slug, 7–8, 37, 40, 49, 53, 58, 114, 137, 145, 149
snake, 40, 53, 115, 145
snail, 10, 37, 38, 58, 137, 145, 155; sea, 157, 162, 163–6, 197, 200, necklace shell, 194, violet, 190; water, 70, 76, 81, 85, 100, 103, 105, 108, great pond, 70, 104, Jenkins' spire shell, 76, 81, ramshorn, 70, 81, wandering, 70
sparrow, house, 15, 18; hedge *see* dunnock
sparrow-hawk, 114
spider, 10, 37, 38, 40, 41, 50–1, 57, 58, 149; crab, 154–5; water, 99
spindle, 123

sponge, 192, 193
springtail, 37–8
squirrel, 8, 40, 56, 119
starfish, 165, 169, 181, 194, 197, 201
starling, 18–19, 137
starwort, 68, 69
stickleback, 9, 61, 95–6, 98
stoat, 114, 145, 146, 147, 148
stonefly, 76, 105, 107
sycamore, 20, 123

thin tellin, 175–6
thistle, 31, 115, 138
thrush, 58, 126, 155
tit, 8, 14–15, 22, 119; blue, 14–15, 141
tides, 11, 157–8, 185, 202
toad, 8, 40, 52–3, 95, 145
toadstool, 34
top shell, 165
treecreeper, 8, 138–9
trout, 75, 97

viper, 115, 147, 148, 149
vole, 8, 10, 55, 114, 145, 147, 149; water, 55, 94

wader, 174, 179; *see also* under individual headings

wagtail, grey, 95; pied, 142
walnut, 117
wasp, 41, 44, 45–6, 126, 153–4
water boatman, 9, 72, 99; -crowfoot, 68; -flea, 66, 74, 99–100; -lily, 68, 77, 80; -louse, 73, 100, 107; -measurer, 84; -milfoil, 69; -soldier, 69
wayfaring tree, 119, 123
weasel, 144, 145, 146, 147, 148
weever, 53, 171; lesser, 179, 198
weevil, 42
whelk, 192–3; dog, 164, 165–6, 193
shitethroat, 141–2
winkle, 157, 163–5, 187, 202
wigeon, 19
wood sorrel, 110
woodlouse, 10, 37, 41, 58, 73, 194, 195
worm, aquatic, 87, 107, sea, 159, 170, 173, 197, 200, sandmason, 176; earth, 8, 37, 38–9, 40, 58, 87, 137, 149
wrack, bladder, 164, 185, 187, 188; channelled 185, 186; flat, 186–7; knotted, 164, 185, 187, 188; saw, 185, 188, 197
wren, 141

yellowhammer, 138

208